"Scripture is a strange book that tel[...]
It feels strange to hear that priesth[...]
this life, so full of work stress, brok[...]
But Welch shows us that being near to God, secured by the priestly [...]
of our Lord Jesus Christ, is what we were made for. This book will help
you see yourself in this strange, wonderful light."

   Jeremy Pierre, Lawrence and Charlotte Hoover Associate Professor
   of Biblical Counseling; Chair, Department of Biblical Counseling
   and Family Ministry, The Southern Baptist Theological Seminary;
   author, *The Dynamic Heart in Daily Life* and *God with Us: A
   Journey Home*

"You have your grace books and your older holiness books. At times,
they exist in two different worlds. Not for Ed Welch. In a book full of rich
insights that link the Old and New Testaments, Welch paints a picture
of holiness and intimacy with God that makes you want to be holy. He
widens our view of holiness, working to craft it into a vision of beauty.
You'll want to obey after reading this book."

   Paul Miller, Executive Director, seeJesus; author, *A Praying Life*
   and *J-Curve*

"There is no greater human longing than for relational intimacy. This
is because we are created for intimacy with our Creator and others. Sin
destroys this intimacy, and the gospel restores it. The best news we will
ever hear is that the perfectly holy God invites us into table fellowship
as his adopted children. By faith every believer has full access as priests
to boldly approach the throne of grace. Ed Welch offers great help in
understanding these astounding results of the finished work of our Great
High Priest. I hope this book has a great influence in encouraging God's
people to seize our priestly privileges in Christ."

   K. Erik Thoennes, Professor and Chair of Theology, Talbot School
   of Theology, Biola University; Elder of Congregational Life, Grace
   Evangelical Free Church, La Mirada, California

"'You are a royal priest. That reality will change how you live.' With this huge claim, Ed Welch introduces *Created to Draw Near*. I wanted to be persuaded, but I was doubtful. My doubts have now been blown away. How did I not see the significance and influence of this truth before? This book will indeed change the way you live by changing your view of God, yourself, and the gospel."

David Murray, Professor of Old Testament and Practical Theology, Puritan Reformed Theological Seminary

"I treasure Ed Welch's writings. I don't know another counselor who can write a book like this—Ed has built for us a rich biblical theology of God's presence. *Created to Draw Near* helped me to understand my Old Testament better, and it grew my love for Jesus as Savior and High Priest of my soul."

Deepak Reju, Pastor of Biblical Counseling and Family Ministry, Capitol Hill Baptist Church; author, *On Guard* and *The Pastor and Counseling*

"When some writers and preachers today suggest that the gospel is only about forgiveness, Ed Welch reminds us that it is also good news that God brings us into a life of holiness."

Gerald McDermott, Anglican Chair of Divinity and Director of the Institute of Anglican Studies, Beeson Divinity School, Samford University

CREATED TO
DRAW NEAR

Other Crossway books by Edward T. Welch

Caring for One Another: 8 Ways to Cultivate Meaningful Relationships (2018)

Side by Side: Walking with Others in Wisdom and Love (2015)

CREATED TO DRAW NEAR

OUR LIFE AS GOD'S ROYAL PRIESTS

EDWARD T. WELCH

CROSSWAY®

WHEATON, ILLINOIS

Trade paperback ISBN: 978-1-4335-6638-7
ePub ISBN: 978-1-4335-6641-7
PDF ISBN: 978-1-4335-6639-4
Mobipocket ISBN: 978-1-4335-6640-0

Library of Congress Cataloging-in-Publication Data

Names: Welch, Edward T., 1953- author.
Title: Created to draw near : our life as God's royal priests / Edward T. Welch.
Description: Wheaton : Crossway, 2020. | Includes bibliographical references and index.
Identifiers: LCCN 2019019519 (print) | ISBN 9781433566387 (tp)
Subjects: LCSH: Priesthood, Universal. | Identity (Psychology)–Religious aspects–Christianity.
Classification: LCC BT767.5 .W45 2020 (print) | LCC BT767.5 (ebook) | DDC 234–dc23
LC record available at https://lccn.loc.gov/2019019519
LC ebook record available at https://lccn.loc.gov/2019980346

Crossway is a publishing ministry of Good News Publishers.

LB   30   29   28   27   26   25   24   23   22   21   20
15   14   13   12   11   10   9   8   7   6   5   4   3   2   1

To

Ruby	Adelaide
Weston	Alden
Jasper	Jack
Penny	Lucy

Each of you, an inspiration

Contents

Will God indeed dwell with man on the earth?[1]

Let everyone, therefore, who knows
himself to be a Christian,
be assured of this, that we are all equally priests.[2]

The proper condition of creatures,
is to keep close to God.[3]

Introduction

Longing for Closeness

Our independent streak runs deep. Our desire for closeness runs deeper.

- A baby stops crying when held.

- Children want to be part of a group and have a best friend.

- Face-to-face always beats digital communication.

- To be truly known, with nothing to hide, and to truly know others is life at its best.

- Loneliness is the worst. Solitary confinement remains the most intolerable of punishments. Even a child's short timeout can feel unbearable.

- When close to death, we want other people to be with us. No one wants to die alone.

The human condition is bent toward connection and closeness. We know that close relationships with other people are hard, and they can hurt us deeply, but we don't give up. Even after being devastated we still hold out hope that a close relationship is possible. Substitutes for these relationships—things and activities—always fall short.

Go a little deeper, and we notice something similar even toward God. We might prefer him at a safe distance—a distant God makes fewer demands on us—but we want him close during trouble and might be frustrated when he seems quiet at such times, though we might have ignored him for months. Even atheists have their moments. Julian Barnes, in *Nothing to Be Frightened Of*, wrote of his attempt to face his fear of death, "I don't believe in God, but I miss him."[4]

To be close to God is certainly a human desire, but intimacy with someone you can't see has its challenges, and intimacy when you feel a bit guilty is even more challenging. This intimacy, however, is *the* Christian hope, and we will not give up on it.

All this carries the stamp of our spiritual lineage: we are priests. God's intent for humanity has been that we would live in his house and receive his divine hospitality.[5] That is the mission of the priests—*priests are near God.* From that starting point, we will accumulate rich details. In his royal residence, which he declares is also our own, we are known, unashamed, at peace with each other, dressed in garments he himself tailored, ushered into a feast, and joined to him in communion that leaves us searching for words to describe. This priestly identity is a premiere way of understanding God's people—*all* God's people, male and female.

In order to enter in, Scripture must shape the priesthood for us because we all come with memories and images of priests—some good, some odd, some horrible. Many of us want to avoid priests who are wearing full regalia. They are different from the rest of us. When they are near, levity comes to an end, which suggests that God, too, opposes fun. They can use their authority for their own purposes, which poisons the entire priesthood and dishonors God. So we must understand our-selves as priests by how God identifies the priesthood rather than how we experience priests past and present.

Once you try on this identity, you will enjoy wearing it. Just imagine: the priests served in God's house, knew God close up, ate meals with him, and enjoyed his presence. When they circulated among the people, they had the enviable job of pronouncing a blessing over them:

> The LORD bless you and keep you;
> the LORD make his face to shine upon you and
> be gracious to you. (Num. 6:24–25)

What's not to like? And this is just for starters.
You are a royal priest. That reality will change how you live.

PART 1

OUR PAST

EDEN

> God
> Heaven
> Temple
> **NEAR**
> Eden
> Earth
> Humanity

In the Garden of God

A natural way to follow the priestly story is to look for tabernacles and temples. This is where priests worked, and this is where God came near. In Israel's history, the tabernacle was God's portable tent, assembled during the wilderness years. The temple refers to the stationary dwelling of God in Jerusalem that came later. They both identify God's house on earth.

Figure 1 illustrates the layout of the original tabernacle. It consisted of an enclosed, two-room tent with an outer courtyard. The innermost room of the tent was the Most Holy Place, and this was where humanity came closest to the Lord. It was designed as a 15 foot by 15 foot square (4.5 meters). If you include the covering, it was a perfect cube. It was God's throne room and the place of his presence. Access was restricted to one visit a year by the high priest. The adjacent room, with its less than perfect rectangular design (15 feet by 30 feet), was entered daily by one of the priests who cared for a lamp and an altar that burned incense. Outside the tent was an open courtyard, which was always a buzz of activity. Surrounding all this were heavy curtains 7 feet high, 75 feet wide, and 150 feet long.

Figure 1   The Wilderness Tabernacle (Exodus 25–30)

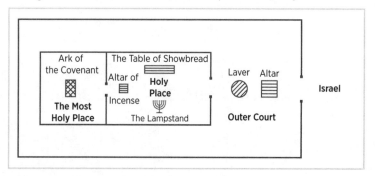

The problem is that the tabernacle doesn't appear until later in Scripture's unfolding story—around the time of Moses. Identities are forged at creation. So we look for times when God came near *before* the tabernacle.

> In the beginning, God created the heavens and the earth. The earth was without form and void, and darkness was over the face of the deep. And the Spirit of God was hovering over the face of waters. (Gen. 1:1–2)

God's realm is heaven, and man's is earth, which is why the Spirit's hovering over the waters is unexpected. Hovering implies closeness. Eagles hover over their young (Deut. 32:11). The gods of legends stayed in their abodes. The one true God, however, came close, and when he did, the life of heaven came to earth. It did in the beginning. It did when the Spirit "overshadowed" Mary (Luke 1:35). It did later when the Spirit descended on Jesus at his baptism (Luke 3:22). It does now. Apparently, heaven was never meant to contain the triune God. The movement between heaven and earth was always intended to be fluid.

What follows is the story of that movement between heaven and earth—God coming from his abode into our own, and we being brought into his. Here you will find priests. It is an intensely personal story of mutual engagement. The question is, How will the holy God come close to his unholy people, make them his own, and be with them in the most intimate of ways? It will happen. The hovering Spirit heralded what was to come.

Within Eden was a garden—lush, with no hint of death or unfruitful foliage. Everywhere there was rich, lively, almost-too-much-to-bear life. It could be no other way because this was the garden of God, the place where heaven and earth met. It was a "trysting place" more than a mere garden.[6] Here God and humanity went for a walk. This was "the holy mountain of God" that later generations hoped to gather around and perhaps ascend (Ezek. 28:14). This was God's house.

For the ancient Israelites the reference was clear: the garden was the first tabernacle, and humanity's home was in the presence of God, in his Most Holy Place. The evidence is unmistakable (figure 2).[7] Wherever God is, *there* is the tent of his dwelling.

Figure 2   The First Tabernacle in Eden (Genesis 2)

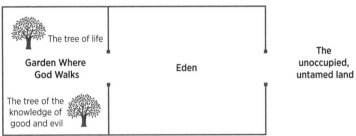

And the LORD God planted a garden in Eden, in the east, and there he put the man whom he had formed. And out of the ground the LORD God made to spring up every tree that is pleasant to the sight and good for food. The tree of life was in the midst of the garden, and the tree of the knowledge of good and evil. A river flowed out of Eden to water the garden, and there it divided and became four rivers. . . . The LORD God took the man and put him in the garden of Eden to work it and keep it. (Gen. 2:8–10, 15)

- The word *garden* itself suggests something enclosed and protected. It was set apart from everything else. The garden was *in* Eden. Eden was a larger demarcated area, and then there was the world beyond. The heavenly template for the tabernacle was already in view: the holy place (Eden) was *near* him; the Most Holy Place (the garden) was *nearer*.

- Since God is life, we can expect to see water close by. "A river flowed out of Eden to water the garden, and there it divided and became four rivers" (Gen. 2:10). These rivers appear again both in Ezekiel's vision of the temple (Ezek. 47:1–12) and in John's vision with "the water of life, bright as crystal, flowing from the throne of God and of the Lamb" (Rev. 22:1).

- Humanity had a mission in this tabernacle—"to work it and keep it" (Gen. 2:15)—which is the same language used for the priests and Levites in Israel's tabernacle. The priests were to serve and "keep guard" over it (Num. 1:53; 3:36). This means that humanity's work in the garden was not restricted to gardening. Humanity was to maintain the temple grounds and also protect it from intruders.

- Among Eden's foliage was the tree of life. It may have been the means by which the Lord actually gave his people lasting life. It was also designated as a symbol of the life we have in God's presence. God always connects the life we can have in him with a sign. In the next version of the tabernacle, the tree will be a stylized version of itself, taking the form of a flowering lampstand (Ex. 25:31–34), merging the images of life and light. Later, in the final temple, the tree is no longer partitioned but is available through Jesus to all the nations and is intended for their healing (Rev. 22:1–2).

All this means that from the beginning, our everyday existence was intended to be lived out in the temple precincts. Our heritage is the royal priesthood. And since God's purposes for us have never changed, you are a royal priest. You have a rich job description, and his Spirit is with you. God's fellowship and hospitality have begun in earnest.

For now, imagine this priesthood as a walk with the Lord. He walked with man and woman in the garden. He continued to walk with unfaithful people in the wilderness and promised, "I will walk among you and will be your God, and you shall be my people" (Lev. 26:12). He desires that we be close. This certainly can erode old myths of God being far off and chronically disappointed with you.

Communion. Closeness. Heaven comes to earth, and our home is at the intersection of the two. This has been God's plan for humanity, and he has done it.

Response

In keeping with the personal back-and-forth communication we can have with God himself, it seems natural to respond.

1. There is a difference between being set loose in a nice garden and being placed close to God in his house on earth. What difference does that make for the way you tell your own story?

2. You learn a lot about people by spending time in their house. As you enter this early house, the garden, what do you learn about the Lord?

2

In God's Image

We are created in God's own image.

> Then God said, "Let us make man in our image, after our likeness." (Gen. 1:26)

Never has so much been packed into one phrase. To bear his image is to be like him and have the capacity to grow in a relationship with him. Nearness, after all, is useless if there is not a similarity of one to the other. We can enjoy the presence of a dog or a cat, and pets can sometimes touch our loneliness, but a pet can't replace someone of our own kind.

Animals, like *all* creation, reflect God's glory and bear his likeness. There is something about their strength, their communities, and their unique abilities that point to God. Light, water, and rocks do the same. They reflect God's glory and are like him in some way. Humanity, however, stands out. Whereas all subhuman creation reflects God, we are like him in every way a creature can be like him.

For those coming out of Egypt, the first to hear of this image bearing, the news was electric. They had heard that only

Pharaoh imaged a god and had access to the gods; the rest were Pharaoh's servants or slaves. But then an entire slave nation was told that they shared a unique connection to the God who is over all gods. As children are to the father, so they were to God. A "chip off the ol' block"—that's what "in the image" communicated. This familial connection was affirmed when the same language was used for Adam's relationship with his offspring. "When Adam had lived 130 years, he fathered a son in his own likeness, after his image" (Gen. 5:3).

We experience a likeness or kinship to God that uniquely qualifies us for a relationship with him. We can represent him to the world, we can participate in his purposes, and we can imitate him. Of all creation, we share the closest kinship with God, so we alone can know him and be known by him in the most intimate of ways. We alone can have back-and-forth communication that is reserved for personal relationships. Our connection is more intense. We, distinct from all else, can know his love and love him in return. We alone have the capacity to live in God and he in us—a reality that became central to the apostle Paul's teaching. No wonder the psalmist identifies us as having been crowned with glory and honor (Ps. 8:5).

So, as it turns out, priests are the very offspring of God and share in his likeness. Our lineage is from heaven, which makes us hybrids of heaven and earth, though the scales tip in the direction of heaven. We are more connected to heaven than is the rest of creation. We are children priests or, since our Father is the king, we are royal priests who can enjoy his companionship as he actually enjoys ours.

From that Edenic home we—humanity—were sent out, as if our home were also a staging site for our priestly mission. There was much to do. The world beyond Eden was untamed, and we were called to claim it for the Lord, work it, and keep it. Our mission was to imitate him and represent him on earth. We are angled mirrors capable of reflecting his glory to the world, which assumes that we need his presence; otherwise there is nothing to reflect. With our eyes on him, we learn his ways and then imitate him.

Life giving captures it. Fruitful. Humanity blesses the earth and extends the life of God to its farthest reaches—"Be fruitful and multiply and fill the earth and subdue it" (Gen. 1:28). This means that man's purpose was to expand the boundaries of the garden and raise up new priests to represent the Lord throughout the earth. Later, the mission was summarized as "be holy, for I am holy" (e.g., Lev. 11:45)—this too identifies people as agents of life. Later still, Jesus supplanted it with the Great Commission: "Go, therefore, and make disciples of all nations, baptizing them in the name of the Father and of the Son and of the Holy Spirit" (Matt. 28:19). The New Testament writers simplify the Great Commission as a call to reflect and embody the love of Jesus. Heaven comes to earth *through us*, through Spirit-powered love. And in the midst of it all, we enjoy fellowship as we participate in God's plans and are further brought into his love. This is life in its fullness.

Humanity was given a heady and noble mission indeed, one that would benefit from some experience and maturity. As a result, before heading farther east and carrying the Lord's emblem to new lands, humanity needed to be readied by way of a little testing and training.

Response

1. You can certainly be sobered by this revelation of being made in God's image. It carries significant responsibilities. But for now, your task is to be elevated by it. You are the King's offspring on earth—an identity filled with honor. This adds meaning to everything. In the details of life, you live out your

royal calling. Are you lifted up by this? And how does this make a difference in daily life?

2. Receiving abundant life and giving life are significant features of your story. Take some time to recognize it. When have you known life? When have you seen it in others? At this point in the biblical storyline, we can already anticipate that giving and receiving life will find its fullest expression in Jesus, who is the way, the truth, and the life.

3

Not Yet Dressed

The first priests were naked, at least for a time.

Young children seem to enjoy being naked. My daughter would babysit for a family whose children designated four to five o'clock every afternoon as "Naked Hour." When I first heard this, I thought it odd until I realized that our children and our grandchildren had their own versions of it; they simply hadn't inflicted it on babysitters. First, one three-year-old twin grandson took off some clothes, then the other, then both took off more until there was general hilarity.

The hilarity, however, is reserved for young children, not for adults. Scripture does not identify naked romps through Eden as ideal for humanity. God always intended to dress us, and as we grow up, most of us prefer wearing clothes. So as good as "naked and . . . not ashamed" (Gen. 2:25) might sound to some, the fact of it announced the need for clothing that would come with maturity.[8] This, no doubt, is a relief to most of us.

When kings ascend to their thrones, they wear majestic garments. When priests were installed, they were invested with royal robes (Ex. 28). Think of how royal robes gave honor to Joseph (Gen. 41:42), Mordecai (Est. 6:8, 11), and even the Prodigal Son (Luke 15:22). Brides, too, participate in this tradition. With new status comes new clothes. Adam and Eve were in line for such honor. Their task was to grow in wisdom, and with wisdom would come investiture and robes of righteousness. All this would make humanity more accurate representatives and reflectors of God's glory, and it would draw us even closer to him.

So beauty is part of the priestly package. If we are close to God, it can be no other way. At the time of Adam and Eve, man certainly had dignity and a kind of beauty because of their close connection with the beautiful one. But that beauty was to increase as man grew in wisdom and became properly dressed in garments tailored under God's specific direction. Once given and altered slightly, they would even inspire a song:

> I will greatly rejoice in the LORD;
>> my soul shall exult in my God,
> for he has clothed me with the garments of salvation;
>> he has covered me with the robe of righteousness,
> as a bridegroom decks himself like a priest with a
>>> beautiful headdress,
>> and as a bride adorns herself with her jewels.
>>> (Isa. 61:10)

The path toward this beautification was straightforward: "Of the tree of the knowledge of good and evil you shall not eat" (Gen. 2:17). This was the way toward beauty, honor, and communion with God. Do this and truly live. The path man chose veered from this path, but the beautification project continued nonetheless because it did not rely on man's obedience and best efforts but solely on God's pursuit.

Response

1. Imagine what this beautification means for your insecurities and shame. God dresses his people, and, with this clothing, we have nothing to hide. As the story unfolds, the priests are the first ones to be clothed, and much of what comes later are variations of royal priestly garments (e.g., Eph. 6:10–18). How has God clothed you? What difference does that make?

2. You are a priest who is clothed, and you are a priest who is growing or maturing. The child becomes the adult, and the adult always has room for greater growth and maturity. How do you hope to grow? As we notice even in human relationships, the result is even more intimacy with the Lord.

Discern Right from Wrong

The two trees of Eden tell us much about being priestly and more fully human. The knowledge of good and evil, and our opting for the good, is the way of true life. We disregard these distinctions to our peril. "The tree of the knowledge of good and evil you shall not eat, for in the day that you eat of it you shall surely die" (Gen. 2:17).

It was one simple thing. When God says no, we imitate him and say no. That is the way we look like our God and enter into his fellowship. We could call it distinguishing right from wrong, and it is essential to all relationships. Every relationship has its rules that are intended to bless that relationship. We speak the truth, we keep our word, we have the best interest of the other in our heart. Do these, and a relationship grows. Ignore them, and it dies. This happens in human relationship because it follows the divine pattern.

To be fully human, which means to be close to the Lord, we must know that there are two paths.

The path that is with God and to God is life and honor. It says yes with his yes and no with his no.

The path that leads away from God can feel like pleasure for a moment, but it goes headlong into death. It says yes to his no and no to his yes.

Discernment between these two paths is essential. It is a premiere feature of our humanity. Moral discernment, obedience, knowing right from wrong—these are irrelevant matters to animals and rocks but essential for a fruitful and good life to those who are replicas of the heavenly God on earth.

In order to grow in this most noble task, our Father gives us everything we need. Throughout history he has been open with and specific about the two ways of life, and he has been keen to repeat himself and plead with us to discern the right. By the time of Moses, when the Ten Commandments and many other laws started pouring in, it was as if man could not be trusted with the minutest of decisions, so the Lord spelled them out. But, at first, the direction was kept to a minimum.

"Don't eat from this tree." Why this? It is what good parents do. They teach their children and urge them in obedience for the children's safety and blessing. They urge obedience when they are present or absent, and it is when parents are absent that children's discernment is put to the test. Will they obey only when the parent is watching? Or will the parental direction be understood as good, and will it become part of them? Will children want to live under and with the parent, or will they want to be the parent? Parental direction becomes a test of love, faithfulness, and wisdom.

We face this test in all of our close relationships. Do I really love the other person? Do I genuinely love, or do I love because kindness gets me what I want? Do I love and protect the relationship even when the other person is not present?

But in the garden, why did the Lord use this particular test? Any tree but this one. The test, of course, was perfect. That it doesn't make lots of sense to us is exactly the point. If we obey such tests because we understand them—and agree with God's rationale—we might be trusting in our own understanding. "This makes sense to me. I agree that doing this is in my best interests. Okay. I will not _____ because it will make my life more difficult." In this sort of obedience, God functions as a kind of advisor; the final decision is our own. Much better is the opportunity to know clearly what God says and follow him even when we don't fully understand his reasons.

Consider how this applies to our sexual behavior. Sex is not murder, we reason. We understand that we shouldn't kill people, but consensual sex doesn't hurt anyone, so, in this matter, we will trust ourselves rather than the Lord. In this we perpetuate our own version of the original garden story and lose discernment, which means we lose a significant piece of our humanity, and we lose our priestly nearness.

Our everyday moral decisions are critical. Moral discernment, when honed and practiced, moves us in the direction of our full humanity. It points the way toward the life that is suited to our created design. Obedience, indeed, is a good thing. "For this is the love of God, that we keep his commandments. And his commandments are not burdensome" (1 John 5:3). All this is part of the priestly story because priests are the caretakers of the distinctions between right and wrong.

> To be human—God's priest—is to discern what is best and what is deadly.
>
> To be human is to act on that discernment and obey. This demands confidence in what God says and the humility to place his words above our own understanding and our own desires. It demands faithful love.
>
> To be human is to teach and encourage others in their discernment.

Response

1. Do you see how moral discernment is embedded in our humanity? This means that wisdom and discernment are not only right; they are good. We admire those who keep their anger in check, who are faithful to their word even when it is inconvenient, who speak honestly, and who love. Do you see how obedience is good and is intended to serve the larger purpose of being closer to the Lord?

2. How do you hope to grow in discernment? While in some matters, how to act is clear-cut, such as whether to murder our neighbor or show kindness, in others it is not. Anger, for example, almost always seems right but is almost always wrong. Or how often do you go online and visit sites that you defend as being within bounds but are clearly unhelpful?

5

An Intruder

The serpent is not identified by name in the early stories of Scripture, but we know who he is. He is Satan, the accuser, the evil one. Our world, apparently, has never been completely safe. There has always been chaos in the world that takes effort to subdue. Everyday life was not intended for our relaxation and entertainment.

How telling that Satan took the form of an animal without a personal name. By this time, Satan had traveled a great distance, from a high rank among other created spiritual beings to someone who is almost a something. Though having a certain amount of power, his status had come to rank among the subhuman creatures.

Maybe Adam slipped up even before his conversation with the serpent began, by allowing the serpent to enter a holy place. His job was to keep guard, and this seems to be a serious breach. But there are other places in Scripture where Satan has some access to God's throne room. In Job we read, "There was a day when the sons of God came to present themselves before the LORD, and Satan also came among them" (Job 1:6).

Satan uses times in the heavenly court to accuse humanity and question the ways of God. It happened in Job and again in a vision given to Zechariah, when Satan came prepared to accuse Joshua, a high priest. In neither of these visits was the heavenly court surprised, and there were no attempts to cast him out.

Satan was given occasional access to the inner precincts of God's domain. If he was out of line, he might hear, "The LORD rebuke you" (Zech. 3:2; see also Jude 9), which would have been a fine way for Adam to keep guard. But in the garden the serpent encountered a spiritually drowsy couple. When you have a sneaky enemy, you want to know his habits and characteristic moves, but Adam and Eve were underprepared.

> He [the serpent] said to the woman, "Did God actually say, 'You shall not eat of any tree in the garden'?" (Gen. 3:1)

Satan's first strategy was to imply that God is not good. The serpent massively overstated the original prohibition as a way to entice just the smallest movement in the human's position.

"Your parents are so strict!" A fifteen-year-old student had just mentioned to her friends something about the restrictions on social media in her home, and this was one of the reactions. "It sounds like your mom runs a prison. I couldn't live there."

"Well, I guess my mom is a little strict."

Her mom had discussed the restrictions with her, and the two of them had even decided together on a wise policy. But the reaction from her friend raised small doubts about Mom's goodness.

Satan suggested that God fences you from every good thing and insists on an ascetic lifestyle that majors on self-denial. In other words, "No fun" is the sign over the garden.

His words settled in.

> The woman said to the serpent, "We may eat of the fruit of the trees in the garden, but God said, 'You shall not eat

of the fruit of the tree that is in the midst of the garden, neither shall you touch it, lest you die.'" (Gen. 3:2–3)

The woman corrected the lie. So far so good. But she added, ". . . neither shall you touch it." There it is. The serpent's extreme and blatant lie coaxed her to mildly overstate God's command and question God's goodness. Her response essentially was, "God is not mean. He is just a little stingy, a little picky." The course had been set. Discernment was fading fast, so she was vulnerable to the serpent's next strategy: suggesting that sin is not bad. When you bend the rules, the Serpent suggested, you might rise into new realms of pleasure and insight.

The serpent said to the woman, "You will not surely die. For God knows that when you eat of it your eyes will be opened, and you will be like God, knowing good and evil." (Gen. 3:4–5)

His words, again, left their mark. The tree caught her eye in a new way. The woman saw that "the tree was good for food, and that it was a delight to the eyes, and that the tree was to be desired to make one wise" (3:6). Before priests could protect the holiness of the garden temple, they first had to learn to protect their own hearts.

The serpent's goal is for humanity to be remade in his image and imitate him. His twofold strategy remains his most prominent and effective weapon. Every failed spiritual test can be traced to our tacit agreement with him and these two lies. "Go ahead," he says, "you will like it; rest in your own understanding. Look at the evidence. God is not that good, sin is not that bad. To put it bluntly, God is not good; sin is good."

Even though we know this strategy, we remain vulnerable. With Adam and Eve, all it took was a brief reassessment of the tree. It didn't look dangerous. It even seemed attractive. Our own temptation might coincide with discouragement, hardship, or a bout of hopelessness. Suddenly, the discernment we had yesterday dissolves into a desire to rid ourselves of the bad feelings we have today, and what was once wrong now looks like the perfect remedy.

And the serpent is not quite done. When we follow him into disobedience, Satan will add one final strategy: "You are now irredeemably bad, and God could never forgive or love you." This is a variation on his theme that God is not good, but it has more bite to it. Shame replaces communion and fellowship, and everything is injected with hopelessness. We are fooled into thinking that we can never regain what's been lost.

Response

1. We are, in fact, out of our league. We cannot stand alone before such battle strategies. So we go into training. We examine our hearts. "Test yourselves," writes the apostle Paul (2 Cor. 13:5). When are you most susceptible to Satan's lies?

2. The goodness of God is your critical defense. For the first couple, his goodness is apparent in the walks together, in the lavish provision in the garden, and in the privilege of partnering with God in his mission to the world. For us, the goodness of God is embodied in Jesus and his pursuing love even to death on a cross. How are you prepared to speak of God's goodness when temptations appear?

6

Discernment Lost

Then the LORD God said, "Behold, the man has become like one of us in knowing good and evil. Now, lest he reach out his hand and take also of the tree of life and eat, and live forever."

Genesis 3:22

Humanity experienced a severe loss of status. That's what happens when you follow an animal—you become like the one you follow. You lose part of your humanity. Genesis 3:22, however, suggests that we gained "knowing good and evil" and became more like God. Perhaps it means that humanity had *experienced* good and then evil, but that certainly does not make us like the Lord.

Consider another interpretation of Genesis 3:22: "Behold, the man was like us in knowing good and evil."[9] The original language permits it, and it fits with everything that follows. The man once knew right from wrong—everything was his except that one tree. It was clear. But then the distinctions became muddy because desire rather than careful discernment began to rule the man.

Consider sex again. We might believe that premarital sex is clearly wrong, until we are attracted to someone. Then our discernment becomes muddled, and what was once prohibited seems good. In order to be full-functioning priests we need a steely, moral discernment. To lose it is to become less noble and honorable. It is to become less human. Yet the Lord has determined that nothing will interfere with his priestly call on our lives, so he will do it. He will set us on a course of wisdom and discernment that will culminate in the Spirit of wisdom being poured out on all of us. That wisdom and discernment will be essential for our closeness to God, which is our destiny.

Let's trace this story of discernment. Moses called the people to be the new humanity who discerned right from wrong and followed the Lord:

> See, I have taught you statutes and rules, as the LORD my God commanded me, that you should do them in the land that you are entering to take possession of it. Keep them and do them, for that will be your wisdom and your understanding in the sight of the peoples. (Deut. 4:5–6)

Moses's call went largely unheeded, but the Lord was not done. Later, Solomon gave hope that humanity would flourish as royal priests, when he asked for wisdom to discern:

> "Give your servant therefore an understanding mind to govern your people, that I may discern between good and evil, for who is able to govern this your great people?" It pleased the LORD that Solomon had asked this. (1 Kings 3:9–10; see also 2 Sam. 14:17)

But it didn't last long, as idols soon flooded the land:

> Woe to those who call evil good
>> and good evil,
> who put darkness for light
>> and light for darkness. (Isa. 5:20)

> My people are foolish;
>> they know me not.
> They are stupid children;
>> they have no understanding.
> They are "wise"—in doing evil!
>> But how to do good they know not. (Jer. 4:22)

So the Lord determined to do more. He would send his Son, and the Son would send the Spirit.

> For this is the covenant that I will make with the house of Israel after those days, declares the LORD: I will put my law within them, and I will write it on their hearts. (Jer. 31:33)

Afterward, maturity—being the royal priests he intended us to be—was within reach:

> Solid food is for the mature, for those who have their powers of discernment trained by constant practice to distinguish good from evil. (Heb. 5:14)

Obedience to Christ is not a burden to bear. Instead it points the way to being truly human—an unfettered conscience, an unhindered nearness to him, and the pleasure of his hospitality and protection.

Response

1. When you read "truly human," it means that you are set in a direction that suits who you are. Wisdom and discernment, in other words, enhance life rather than restrict it. Can you give some illustrations in support of this reality?

2. Consider how wisdom and discernment enhance human relationships. Obedience and intimacy travel together. When we speak truth to each other rather than lies, bless rather than curse, or guard our relationship rather than indulge desires that would cause hurt, we grow nearer to the other. How can you bless one of your relationships with more mature discernment? If you don't have any immediate ideas for how to bless one of your relationships, consider a confession of your weaknesses in loving well and your desire to grow in wise love.

7

Life Outside the Most Holy Place

Death had begun its insidious march, and it was much more pervasive than mere physical death. Self-imposed distance in Adam and Eve's relationship with God extended to breaches in their relationship with each other. As death crept into relationships, humanity became blind to personal wrongdoing and magnified the wrongs of others.

> [The Lord] said, "Have you eaten of the tree of which I commanded you not to eat?" The man said, "The woman whom you gave to be with me, she gave me fruit of the tree, and I ate." Then the LORD God said to the woman, "What is this that you have done?" The woman said, "The serpent deceived me, and I ate." (Gen. 3:11–13)

This story is *our* story.

My wife and I were a little late for church. Since we have had a few conflicts about this in the past, I was committed to not blaming her, as that had never gone well. As we arrived at church, I had one thought: don't blame her. Then another couple approached us, and the husband teased me about being a little late, and I said, "Sheri sometimes misjudges how long it takes to get ready." I was thinking one thing, yet the words that came out of my mouth—robotically, automatically—were very different. The only good thing was that I felt horrible, distinctly less than human and ashamed. At least I retained a spark of life, because I was aware that I had just dabbled in death and its relationship-rending ways.

Point and accuse—we do it all the time. We even toss in "the woman you gave me" and blame God himself. Through it all, we can think that we are enlightened as we stand over the perceived culprit in self-righteous judgment (Prov. 14:12).

Look more closely, and the syndrome is actually *hide*, point, and accuse: "Don't look at me. Look at *that* person." The accusations start flying when we want to cover up certain behaviors. So when you blame, consider what you are trying to hide.

At the start, humanity was connected to God and his beauty. Clothes were less critical when we were surrounded by and shared in his majesty. But once we set out on our own, unworthiness invaded everything, and it was experienced as nakedness and as exposure, which is intolerable. Royal investiture became a barely remembered dream.

In response, "the LORD God made for Adam and for his wife garments of skins and clothed them" (Gen. 3:21). This is often seen as evidence of the first sacrifice for forgiveness of sins—and it may well have been—but it is more than that. Among our many spiritual disabilities is that we so quickly forget reality. As a way to jostle a dull memory, the Lord clothed humanity with animal skins. For the ancient Hebrew the message was clear: if you follow an animal, you will look like an animal; if you forsake the path of life, you will wear death.

Among the taboos in Israel was contact with a dead body (e.g., Lev. 11:24). Such contact brought defilement and shame, and the defiled person was separated from the community until a priest offered cleansing. Being draped with a dead animal was no reason for boasting. It was a statement of spiritual need. Man brought ruin to beauty and invited death into the community.

Humanity received what it asked for. We sought independence and life apart from God's words and protection, and we received independence and separation. The work of guarding and keeping the inner garden was left to God's attendants: "[God] drove out the man, and at the east of the garden of Eden he placed the cherubim and a flaming sword that turned every way to guard the way to the tree of life" (Gen. 3:24).

If we read between the lines of what immediately follows, the first family did not travel far from Eden. They knew that life could not thrive apart from the Lord, so they stayed close. Even more, they had somehow learned that a substitute could stand in their place, so, with some divine direction, they established a sacrificial system by which they could approach him: the blood of an animal for the blood of humanity. This became a key insight for God's priests: God will, in fact, accept substitutes in our place.

This early priestly system was imperfect. Everyone knows that an animal cannot bear the guilt and shame of humanity. The system was never intended to rest on the merit and suitability of the animal. It was, instead, grounded on the mercy and forgiving grace of God and the hope that he would make things right.

Meanwhile, humanity's instinct to point at and blame others reached its tragic fulfillment when Abel murdered his brother. Blame is a form of judgment: "I am right; you are wrong." It is a kind of curse: "May you be damned [rather than me]." We want the best for ourselves and punishment to fall on another. Murder was inevitable.

The murderer, Cain, went farther out into Nod, to the east of Eden. Cain left the presence of the Lord and was a fugitive rather than a priest who claimed earth for the Lord. The earth's map was changing (figure 3). Humanity was farther from God's inner room. Yet nothing had changed. God created us to be a priesthood and to live at the meeting place of heaven and earth, and he would do it.

Figure 3   Farther from God's Presence (Genesis 3:21–23)

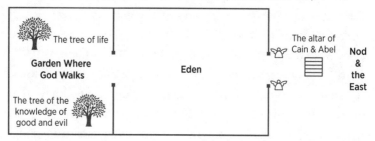

Response

1. Expect pointing and blaming to be almost natural. When we move into the New Testament, we see Jesus address this in an especially vivid manner:

> Why do you see the speck that is in your brother's eye, but do not notice the log that is in your own eye? Or how can you say to your brother, "Let me take the speck out of your eye," when there is the log in your own eye? You hypocrite, first take the log out of your own eye, and then you will see clearly to take the speck out of your brother's eye. (Matt. 7:3–5)

Do you notice any recent logs? Do you see how these logs are just a short step from murder?

2. A law is at work here: what happens in your relationship with God will be expressed in your relationship with people. When you turn from God, you will turn against other people. If you break fellowship with God, you can expect broken relationships with those close to you. How does that law work in your own life?

ISRAEL

Holy
Tabernacle
Altars
Sacrifices
Blood
NEAR
CLOSE
PRESENCE
Clothed
Meals
Blessed
Cleansed

8

Sanctuaries and Ladders

The priestly story gathers more detail after the Edenic catastrophe. Keep an eye out for any time God is close.

Altars. Altars mark the place where heaven came to earth.

God's voice and heavenly visions. When God speaks, he is present, and the natural response is to build an altar or a monument.

Blessings and promises. Both are evidences of life in our midst. They come because God pursues us. When he blesses us, we will, in turn, pass that blessing to others, and a prized priestly job is to pronounce blessings.

Holy. The word *holy* is loaded with meaning. In our common use, it identifies people who are especially obedient and wholehearted in their devotion to the Lord, which suggests that it is a small group. But it actually identifies people, places, special days, and objects that God has brought close to himself.

Priests. Official priests begin to populate the story. Melchizedek suddenly appears and just as suddenly is gone. Others go through more ordinary channels and are ordained for their mission.

Job. Job emerges as one of our priestly ancestors. After his children would gather together for a celebration, he "would send and consecrate them, and he would rise early in the morning and offer burnt offerings" (Job 1:5). Consecration is a way of cleansing and making holy, and offerings on altars were the prescribed way to do such things. Job was a priest, first and foremost.

Abraham. Abraham heard the word of the Lord. He was blessed and fruitful, enabled to live out the original priestly mission to bless the earth. The mission started with land that was set apart for him, his staging site. From there, great things happened. In response, he did what priests do: "He built an altar to the LORD and called upon the name of the LORD" (Gen. 12:8). Through this sacrifice Abraham and his people were cleansed and made suitable occupants for the land, and the land itself was cleansed and prepared for God to dwell with his people.

Melchizedek. Melchizedek appeared (Genesis 14). While following the story of Abraham and looking ahead to the Aaronic line of priests who were Abraham's descendants, we discover that there was an even greater line. Melchizedek was "priest of God Most High" (v. 18), and his reputation preceded him; Abraham gave him a tenth of everything he owned. As God's priest Melchizedek shared in the status of God himself, which means that he was Jesus. Melchizedek's coming and going were brief, but earth was joined to heaven in Melchizedek, who made visits on behalf of the triune God. Otherwise, this priest is what we might expect. He had communion with people by way of a meal of bread and wine; then he blessed them.

Yet we might keep this in mind: this priest met man in a battlefield, after Abraham had routed some local rulers who took some of his possessions. We find priests on battlefields again when they lead Israel into victory over Jericho (Josh. 6). We, too, are priests on a battlefield, though it is against Satan, the enemy of all enemies, and his dominion (Eph. 6:10–18). Our strategy is to fight in the Spirit and take a stand by insisting that we submit to God and his ways (e.g., James 4:7).

Jacob. Melchizedek was clearly identified as a priest. We can't miss him. We can, however, miss Jacob and his dream about a ladder. Abraham's grandson Jacob was on the run from an angry brother and on a journey to find a spouse. While far from home, he settled in for a night's rest, and the Lord gave him a dream:

> He dreamed, and behold, there was a ladder set up on the earth, and the top of it reached to heaven. And behold, the angels of God were ascending and descending on it! And behold, the LORD stood above it and said, "I am the LORD, the God of Abraham your father and the God of Isaac. (Gen. 28:12–13)

Jacob identified the dream accurately: "then Jacob awoke from his sleep and said, 'Surely the LORD is in this place, and I did not know it. . . . This is none other than the house of God, and this is the gate of heaven" (Gen. 28:16–17).

God is in heaven, we are on earth, yet there are times when heaven and earth meet. There is a ladder that joins the two. The Lord stands above it, and his emissaries move easily between the two realms. Heaven is closer to earth than we have thought.

In response, "Jacob took the stone that he had put under his head and set it up for a pillar and poured oil on the top of it. He called the name of that place Bethel" (Gen. 28:18–19). It was only a stone or two, but that's how temples get started. This temple was the house of God, and from it was a ladder that traversed into heaven itself.

The drama was building. The signs were everywhere. When the veil of heaven is pulled back for a moment, as it was with the ladder, we see that much is happening. And God is resolute—he was making a way for his royal priests to be with him. He is never far.

Response

1. Consider again how God wants to be with you. The best of human relationships express this closeness. People want to be together. We love each other, even when we are imperfect. You have seen or experienced this. It exists because humanity reflects some of the glory of God.

2. The priestly life was widely available at this point in biblical history, but we do not yet find illustrations of women functioning as priestly representatives. Scripture indicates that husbands and fathers represent spouses and daughters before the Lord and others, Abigail being one obvious exception (1 Sam. 25). The representative task of the men was later given to Jesus alone, who represented us all, and from there the priestly calling was redistributed. No one is left behind in this calling. So even though, at this point in the biblical story, refinements and additions were still to come to the priestly identity, you can begin now to envision what shape this takes in your own life.

9

Jacob

When tracking our priestly line, Jacob stands out twice. The first time is when he left home both to escape his brother's anger and to look for a suitable wife. This is when he had the dream of the ladder to heaven. The second time is when he left his father-in-law Laban, family in tow, and prepared for a meeting with his brother Esau and Esau's sizeable militia. Jacob was expecting the worst. This is when God descended for the evening and Jacob wrestled with God.

The event is unparalleled in Scripture, so it is difficult to understand.[10] But we know this: priests are the ones brought close to God, and Jacob was very close:

> Jacob was left alone. And a man wrestled with him until the breaking of the day. When the man saw that he did not prevail against Jacob, he touched his hip socket, and Jacob's hip was put out of joint as he wrestled with him. Then he said, "Let me go, for the day has broken." But Jacob said, "I will not let you go unless you bless me." And he said to him, "What is your name?" And he said, "Jacob." Then he said, "Your name shall no longer be

called Jacob, but Israel, for you have striven with God and with men, and have prevailed." Then Jacob asked him, "Please tell me your name." But he said, "Why is it that you ask my name?" And there he blessed him. So Jacob called the name of the place Peniel, saying, "For I have seen God face to face, and yet my life has been delivered." (Gen. 32:24–30)

Prior to this event, the ladder to and from heaven had been quite active. Angels had come to Jacob after the difficult meeting with Laban, and Jacob had just prayed his first recorded prayer, which was beautiful—words from earth to heaven (Gen. 32:9–12). It was marked by humility and praise to God rather than by his normal trickster style. The critical pieces of this story follow.

Jacob was alone, and it was dark. This is scary enough, but the imminent danger to his family posed by Esau makes this a watershed moment for Jacob. Would he and his family survive the next twenty-four hours?

God met him. God responds to our fears. Throughout Scripture the Lord assured his people of his presence during precarious times. In this story, Jacob understood that God was in heaven, which was close enough to be seen. He also knew that God comes even closer in dreams and visitations to earth. Yet no one could have anticipated that God would come this close.

God emptied himself of strength. It was Jesus himself who came to Jacob, and we get a glimpse of how Jesus would later empty himself of power, all for our advantage. Otherwise, a close encounter with him would be devastating to human beings.

God revealed his strength gently. The evening of wrestling was not enough to open Jacob's eyes to the Lord. But Jacob saw clearly after the brief touch that permanently injured his hip. God and his strength were revealed. Unexpected is this: the typical response to a close encounter with the God of power is some trembling and falling down before him in a posture that is part worship and part plea for mercy (e.g., Luke 8:47). Yet Jacob kept right on wrestling and insisted on a blessing. In other words, those who know God accurately know that he is inclined to be near, and to be near is to bless.

God blessed him. With Jacob still clinging to "the man," the Lord blessed him with a new name—Israel. "Deceiver"— the meaning of Jacob—was no longer going to define him. He had lived by his wits, but now he would live as "Prevailer with God." He actually met face-to-face with God, clung to him, and received God's favor. The change in his name was the blessing.

Priests typically were models of decorum when they came near to the Lord. There were, however, especially desperate times during which they learned that they could not make life work through their own cunning. At those times desperation emboldened them. Like the impudent midnight caller who kept asking a neighbor for bread until he finally got out of bed and gave him bread (Luke 11:5–8), we have the option of holding on to the Lord even tighter as we remember his power and love. There is more than one way to be near and receive the blessing he promises.

Response

1. The biblical priestly story is only beginning, and already we discover that heaven is quite close and the stairway between the two is very busy. Scripture is giving you eyes to see. What are you seeing?

2. What might be your own version of wrestling with God? More desperate troubles are an occasion for the Lord to draw us in.

10

Moses

Jacob did not have to display his priestly credentials because the regulated priesthood did not yet exist. But by the time we get to Moses, it did. God's priests were condensed to include men from the tribe of Levi. They had to come from the right family line, be the right age, and have no obvious physical disabilities. Moses's story, therefore, begins with him being connected to Jacob's third son, Levi.

Of interest to us is that Levites worked in the tabernacle courts, but they couldn't get as near to the Most Holy Place as the priests who descended from Aaron. Moses and Aaron came from Levi, but Moses did not come from Aaron. Since Moses clearly came close to the Lord—closer than any Aaronic priest—he is a small reminder that noncredentialed people like us might also be able to come near to God, and he might come near to us.

His story begins this way: "Now a man from the house of Levi went and took as his wife a Levite woman" (Ex. 2:1). In other words, this couple would have a priestly son, and he would stand in the gap between heaven and earth. He would receive words from the Lord to give to the people, and he would hear the pleas of the people to give to the Lord. In Moses, humanity's true identity would become more vivid than in anyone before Jesus. Following are three priestly episodes from his life.

1. *Meeting God in a bush*. While living in the wilderness, settled with a growing family but on the run from Egypt, Moses led the flock of sheep he was tending to the base of Horeb, "the mountain of God" (Ex. 3:1).

> And the angel of the Lord appeared to him in a flame of fire out of the midst of a bush. He looked, and behold, the bush was burning, yet it was not consumed. And Moses said, "I will turn aside to see this great sight, why the bush is not burned." When the Lord saw that he turned aside to see, God called to him out of the bush, "Moses, Moses!" And he said, "Here I am." Then he said, "Do not come near; take your sandals off your feet, for the place on which you are standing is holy ground." (Ex. 3:2–5)

Here was a moveable Most Holy Place. Wherever God is, there is holy ground. With Moses, God came to earth and appeared in a flame of fire, but the bush was not consumed. In other words, the consuming fire, who is not to be trifled with, is also the life who gently cleanses and purifies, and he invites us to draw near.

No doubt Moses needed cleansing in order to be safe in God's presence. In this visitation, cleansing was symbolized in the removal of sandals. Feet, especially dirty feet, were a focal point in that culture. It was shameful to come into someone's home with sandals still on. Uncleanness was to be left at the door. Later, and more deeply, the Lord washed our uncleanness so that we can be with him without shame.

The Lord and Moses had a conversation.

First, the Lord spoke.

Then Moses spoke.

Then the Lord spoke.

Then Moses spoke (Ex. 3:4–4:17).

This is an image-bearing priest on grand display. We alone are like God in such a way that he speaks to us, we listen, we speak to him, and he listens—back and forth. This is what can happen when God comes close, and it was a distinctive feature of Moses's life.

2. *Meeting God on a mountain.* When Moses led the people out of Egypt, he was invited again to speak with the Lord. This time heaven and earth met at Mount Sinai. Though there is no mention of a ladder, the mountain itself was the ladder. Moses ascended and descended the mountain a number of times, first by himself, then with Aaron, then with seventy of the elders. When the elders were invited, they were given a glimpse of heaven itself. "There was under his feet as it were a pavement of sapphire stone, like the very heaven for clearness" (Ex. 24:10), and there they ate and drank with the Lord. But there was the possibility of being even closer.

Only Moses was invited farther up. The elders would stop at the early version of the tabernacle's Holy Place. Moses would ascend into the Most Holy Place. He went up onto the cloud-covered mountain for six days. On the seventh day the Lord spoke with him (Ex. 24:16). The scene is unmistakable. God's intention to be with his people was expressed in earnest. Moses was the new Adam. On the seventh day Adam had walked with the Lord, and these walks were reconstituted with Moses.

On his final ascent of the mountain, Moses was with the Lord for forty days. Whether it was the sheer amount of time they spoke or the fuller presence of the Lord, Moses was obviously transformed by their conference. "And behold, the skin of his face shone" (Ex. 34:30). When you are invited to come close, you become more brilliant and shiny, because the Lord is the light.

3. *Meeting God in a small tent.* After this final ascent, the Lord descended further and came to Moses at the tent of meeting. This tent was pitched outside the camp, at a safe distance from the people. It was the forerunner to the first tabernacle, and "tent of meeting" was sometimes used as the more personal name for the tabernacle. There "the LORD used to speak to Moses face to face, as a man speaks to his friend" (Ex. 33:11).

Moses went on to expand the priestly tasks and privileges.

He established altars and made sacrifices and burnt offerings.

He guarded and kept the temple mountain as a way to protect the people.

He made a stand for God's holiness (Ex. 32:21).

He led people into war (Ex. 17:8).

He taught and applied the words of the Lord to the people (Lev. 10:11; Deut. 33:10).

But it was the presence of God—God's nearness—that identified him as a priest unto the Lord.

Response

1. Moses was such a singular figure, but he "did not receive what was promised, since God had provided something better for us" (Heb. 11:39–40). Somehow, because of Christ and because the Spirit has been given to us, you have what Moses had, and more. What do you have that is better?

2. The exchange between God and Moses at the burning bush seems almost ordinary. It is an early conversation that was later identified as friendship. This plain conversation with God himself is what you were made for. How do you hope to grow in this friendship?

11

A Nation of Priests

Now therefore, if you will indeed obey my voice and keep
my covenant, you shall be my treasured possession among
all peoples, for all the earth is mine; and you shall be to me
a kingdom of priests and a holy nation.

Exodus 19:5–6

The Old Testament priestly line was demarcated and specific.
Jacob's third son through Leah was Levi (Gen. 29:34), and
Levi's tribe was responsible for the care of the tabernacle
(Num. 1–3). The line of Aaron, a later Levite, was designated
as the group to preside over the altar and burnt offerings. They
were the ones who could go through the temple veil and into
the presence of God (Num. 18:5–7). Anyone else who tried to
penetrate the veil would die. So when we imagine Old Testament priests, we think of the Aaronic priesthood.

This seems to leave many out. Priests represented the people, and the high priest actually wore symbols of the people on
his vestments, but the people in general were not priests, and

those who were female were certainly not priests. But we have reason to think that the line of priests was going to expand.

Remember that Moses was a priest who presided at the altar, and he was from Levi but not Aaron. His line included priests who practiced outside the Jerusalem temple. Watch for Abiathar and those connected to him as a way to track this group of priests.[11]

Samuel was not from Levi but was a priest (1 Sam. 16:2). King David's sons were not from Levi but were priests (2 Sam. 8:18). And hadn't all the people already acted as priests when each family sacrificed a Passover lamb, smeared blood on the door, and had a fellowship meal with the Lord (Ex. 12:1–11)? When anyone entered a home through the blood, they enjoyed the protection of God.

It wasn't the temple or Levi that defined the priesthood. The key was holiness, and holiness—an essential condition for priests in which they were chosen by God, set apart for him and cleansed—was going to be available to everyone (Lev. 19:2; 20:7–8).

The people as priests came first. The Levitical priesthood did not replace the people as priests. It simply offered a more concentrated version of priestly life that would eventually be redistributed to all the people.[12] This means that *you* are a treasured possession. Out of all creation, God determined that those whose allegiance is to him are of great worth, and when you have a treasured possession, you keep it close and never let it go.

You are among a kingdom of priests. Men, women, and children wear the priestly garments. As per the original calling, you go out and serve as priests to the nations that are presently far off.

You are brought into a holy nation. You are not holy be- cause you are pure in yourself or closer to perfection than your neighbor. Only God makes us holy. Humility and thanks, therefore, are the natural response of all priests.

> I will make my dwelling among you, and my soul shall not abhor you. And I will walk among you and will be your God, and you shall be my people. (Lev. 26:11–12)

> You shall be called the priests of the LORD;
>> they shall speak of you as the ministers of our God.
>>> (Isa. 61:6)

Response

1. In this priestly calling, you hear echoes of your identity as God's image bearer. It elevates and honors you. You are a treasured possession. Are you feeling elevated yet?

2. Even if you aren't feeling honored quite yet, there is sufficient reason here to give thanks.

12

Holy

When we follow the priests and how God draws us near to himself, *holy* is the word you will encounter more than any other. It identifies days, places, objects, and people—all uniquely set apart *by* the Lord and *for* the Lord. The Sabbath is holy (Gen. 2:3). The burning bush, where God first met with Moses, was holy ground (Ex. 3:5). Aaron was set apart from other Israelites (1 Chron. 23:13). Firstborns were set apart (Ex. 13:12).

In God's classification system, there were three categories to which everything belonged: holy, clean, or unclean. The clean and unclean were sometimes lumped together as *the common.*

> You are to distinguish between the holy and the common,
> and between the unclean and the clean (Lev. 10:10).

Figure 4 illustrates how these distinctions add detail to the model of Eden, and it anticipates the further detail of the up-coming tabernacle. The holy was the realm of the priests who could go nearest the Lord. The clean were the people in good standing who could come to the gates of the tabernacle. The unclean were the pagan nations as well as Israelites who were contaminated by their own behaviors or by contact with something unclean. They were furthest from God's inner room.

Figure 4   Leviticus 10:10: Unclean, Clean, and Holy

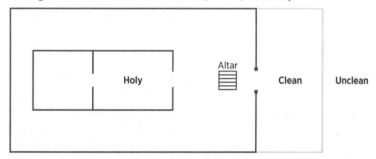

The universe has always been orderly. In the beginning, the Lord moved into the undifferentiated chaos and distinguished between the waters, earth, and sky. These are best kept separate. When they join together, bad things happen, such as floods and hurricanes. We imitate the God of order when we distinguish between incompatible kinds. We work to keep weeds out of grass and flowerbeds. We make dikes and bulkheads to keep oceans separate from land. We put certain animals and bugs outside our homes because, though a domestic dog or cat might be compatible with indoor living, snakes, mosquitos, roaches, and most other animals are among things that live outside.

When this feature of God's style was incorporated into Jewish law, it emerged as sowing a field with a single type of seed or wearing a garment of only one kind of material (Lev. 19:19). These unusual expressions of distinctions and order were a bridge to the deeper order in which God's people were to belong to him and separate themselves from sin. Sin is an alien kind that should not mix with those created in God's image. Death, too, sin's constant companion, is alien to the God of life, so we are not surprised that priestly laws contained taboos against anything that had ties to death. Lobsters and vultures were unclean and prohibited—they were bottom feeders and connected to death. People with skin diseases were unclean and had to be quarantined from the community until they were healed. Mold, a building's version of a skin disease, made a house unclean. If a thorough cleaning didn't work, the house was torn down.

The clean and unclean. Clean is what people hoped for. There was certainly no shame among the clean. They could walk freely among one another. They were free to come and worship at the temple gates and enter the courtyard. They were included. They felt normal, in the best sense, without the nagging thought that there was something wrong with them. But some kind of pollution was always close by, always pulling them toward the unclean, farther from the Lord, closer to death. It came from their own sin, the disobedience of a family member, disease, or inadvertent contact with anything unclean. Left to ourselves, we all slide toward the category of the unclean.

The unclean were farther from God and closer to death. They were excluded from the community because uncleanness was a kind of contagion that infects. The unclean person's only hope was that God would do something to redeem him or her from uncleanness, and he did. The entire sacrificial system was intended to point the way from death toward the life giver himself. The unclean were purified or cleansed. Yet no one could presume once clean, always clean. Vigilance was the order of the day, sacrifices were a regular feature of daily life, and there was hope for something even better.

The holy. Holy things are uniquely associated with God and set apart from the rest of creation. Holy things are near him. They are honorable not because of their intrinsic worth or purity. Rather, they are honorable, because the Lord sets them apart and brings them near to himself.

In the beginning, Eden and the first family were set apart for the Lord, but God left the rest of the world a bit unkempt so humanity could subdue it and gradually bring it within the domain of God's holiness. Then humans rebelled and contaminated the garden, and they were sent farther away. God continued to reclaim what is his. The unclean were made clean, and the clean were made holy. In order to become holy and brought back to God, the once-distant people had to be *consecrated* or *sanctified* (figure 5), which are technical terms that mean "made holy." Blood was inevitably part of this process. A priest smeared or sprinkled blood from a sacrificed animal on whatever was being set apart, such as a house or a person. The blood symbolized life that covered death, but there had to be a death in order to benefit from that life.

Figure 5   The Movement between Unclean, Clean, and Holy

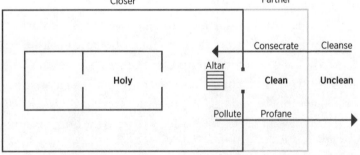

The purpose of humanity is to be brought near to God as a holy people.

As this was displayed in the priesthood, the realities of holiness were brought before people night and day. The message was clear and persistent.

Left to ourselves, we are unclean.

Sin and death (sin's colleague) are our problem.

God has made a way for forgiveness of sins through sacrifice.

His mission is to draw us close to himself and give life.

He takes the unclean and makes them clean.

He takes the clean and makes them holy.

Response

This taxonomy might seem foreign at first. Following are some questions and descriptions that might help.

Unclean

Do you ever feel worthless and excluded?

Do you have thoughts or actions you want to hide?

Does your conscience condemn you?

Do you feel like a fraud? Are you concerned that people will really know you and then reject you?

Do you feel dirty?

Do you feel alone?

Do you think God's promises are for those who are better than you?

Clean

Are there times when you are less self-conscious and simply enjoy what you are doing and who you are doing it with?

Are there times when your conscience doesn't nag you? If so, it doesn't mean you are pure, but it does mean that you have nothing you are trying to hide and are not living in fear of judgment.

Are there times when you believe that the promises of God are actually for you?

Are there times when you believe that you are connected to the Lord because of his love and mercy rather than your own goodness? Clean people know that they need daily cleansing.

Holy

Are you aware that you are not your own but belong to the Lord (e.g., 1 Cor. 6:19–20)?

When you pray, do you ever say, "My Father," or simply, "Father"? This is reserved for those who have believed in the Son and are confident that they have a new relationship with the Father.

Can you say, "Jesus is Lord"? If so, it is evidence of the Holy Spirit working in you.

Do you want to serve others as you have been served and love others as you have been loved? If so, it means that you are being sent from God's house to the world.

Are you ever humbled and thankful as you remember that God has known you by name since the foundations of the earth and that he set you apart because of his commitment to be near you, and not because you have acted holy?

13

A Meal with God

You know that God has accepted you when he invites you to a meal. Among the many plotlines ahead in the biblical story, keep an eye out for God coming down, people going up, and meals. These develop and extend the priestly story. At the Passover, God shared a meal with families and friends, though his presence was not visible. Next, the elders of Israel ascended *to* him and shared a meal:

> Then Moses and Aaron, Nadab, and Abihu, and seventy of the elders of Israel went up, and they saw the God of Israel. There was under his feet as it were a pavement of sapphire stone, like the very heaven for clearness. And he did not lay his hand on the chief men of the people of Israel; they beheld God, and ate and drank. (Ex. 24:9–11)

By this time Israel knew that they could not make their own rules for approaching the Lord. That would court disaster. God was specific about how people could come to him, so there could be no improvisation. God was committed to drawing near and having his people draw near, and there was only one way. These intersecting teachings were expressed both in clear barriers between the people and God and in an invitation for the representatives of Israel to come closer.

And closer they went, on Mount Sinai, the mountain of his presence. The elders did not see the Lord in his fullness—his feet were more than enough—but they were certainly brought into his house. There, under his protection, they beheld him and ate. They enjoyed divine hospitality. These men did not tote their bag lunches and wine up the mountain. God invited, prepared the food, and hosted (figure 6).

Figure 6   Mt. Sinai as God's House (Exodus 24)

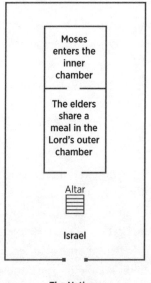

A homemade meal remains the standard for hospitality and fellowship. A most memorable meal was one to which my wife and I were invited. The invitation had come out of a casual conversation on a Saturday morning, and when we arrived that evening, the host couple had been preparing food all day and seemed to have enjoyed the process. When we sat down to eat, there were no distractions, just excellent food, the best of friends, fine conversation, and a shared awareness that life could not get much better.

"Come, live under my protection, enjoy a meal with me; it is my honor to treat you; let's talk." That's the gist of the Lord's Table. It gets to the heart of priestly privileges and pleasures, and it is a recurring event where heaven and earth meet.

There were many more meals. Priests shared a meal from the sacrifices presented to the Lord (Lev. 2:1–16; 3:1–17; 5:14–7:10). People who brought a peace offering shared in a meal with the Lord from that offering. Those who remained faithful to the Lord received an invitation to a soul-satisfying and free banquet (Isa. 55:1–6). And Jesus himself gathered the most unlikely and unworthy to eat with him. But in the days of Moses, the meal was restricted. The elders were invited to God's outer apartment, but only Moses was invited into the inner apartment of God's mountain home.

This was the home first seen in Eden, and it would soon be revealed in more detail. At Mount Sinai, it was configured vertically rather than horizontally. The people were kept at a safe distance. Moses erected an altar at the base. The seventy elders were invited up the mountain where they actually saw the Lord, but only Moses was invited further in. The cloud of the Lord's glory then appeared on Sinai for six days. On the seventh day, Moses went up into the cloud and remained for forty days.

The people saw the cloud of God's glory on the mountain. The elders saw his feet. Moses saw his back (Ex. 33:23). And us? We have seen Jesus, yet there is even more to come. "For now we see in a mirror dimly, but then face to face" (1 Cor. 13:12).

Response

1. A meal is important. Priests ate before the Lord and enjoyed his provision in the tabernacle. The God of the heavens invites you not as a prize for good behavior but out of his intention from the beginning of time to draw you near. Do you believe this? If not, what will it take to believe? If you do, how does this reality reshape you?

2. If you are reluctant to believe, the problem might be a blend of shame and pride: you are ashamed because of your sins or your sense of worthlessness; you are too proud to come to a banquet empty-handed. Toss that aside for the moment and simply come. God is delighted to host, and you need him. He invites; you come (Isa. 55:1–3). How might you come?

14

In God's House

And let them make me a sanctuary, that I may dwell in their midst. Exactly as I show you concerning the pattern of the tabernacle, and of all its furniture, so you shall make it.

Exodus 25:8–9

We know people much better when we are invited into their homes. The pictures, the decorations, and the furniture all reveal something about the hosts. And when the hosts have designed the entire house and contents, *everything* reveals something about them. The tabernacle is the first home in which God gives us so much detail, and it was built for hospitality.

Eden was God's home—it was all about life and communion. Mount Zion was God's home—it was about sacrifices, meals, communion, and promises made to his people and directions for how to be his people. Later, a portable tent or tabernacle became his home. His people were living in tents, and he was going to join them.

The floor plans of God's homes are similar, as they are all based on a heavenly template (figure 7). This home consisted of a tent, surrounded by a courtyard, which was surrounded by the people of Israel, and beyond them was the world that needed the God of Israel.

Figure 7   The Wilderness Tabernacle (Exodus 25–30)

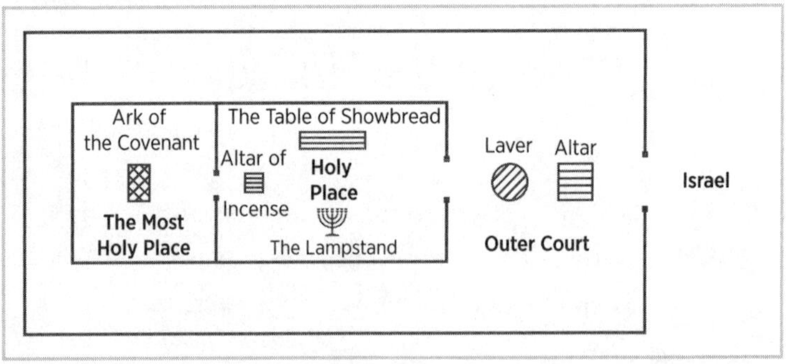

In the tent was God's inner chamber—the Most Holy Place. It was located farthest from the entrance, and the rest of his house supported this particular room. The Most Holy Place connected to an adjacent apartment, often called the Holy Place. It was a kind of antechamber or receiving room, which was maintained daily by an assigned priest. In the surrounding courtyard the priests performed their duties and presented sacrifices. Here the people could come.

Each area, though minimalist, contained details that invite inspection. This is where the priests worked and served (Ex. 25–27).

As priests approached the tabernacle, they saw a 7-foot surrounding wall of fine white linen. The entrance curtain was distinct, with multicolored stitching that was suitable for a king's tent. When priests entered the outer courtyard, the sky itself was the ceiling. It was decidedly earthly—no special floor, no gold. The first object they saw was the bronze altar on which sacrifices were continually offered. The way into the tabernacle necessitated passing the altar, from which blood and death filled the senses.

The problem was clear: the people needed to be forgiven and cleansed before going into God's house. The solution was also clear: God would accept a substitute or representative in their place. Less clear is how this all worked. An animal is living, like us, but is categorically different from us. Whereas we are of heaven and earth, animals are distinctly earthbound. Why God accepted an animal substitute, we do not understand, but we are thankful that he did. Only later will we see how the altar and, indeed, every detail of the tabernacle were facets of Jesus and him crucified.

Farther in, though still in the outer courtyard, was a bronze laver or basin with water for cleansing (Ex. 30:17–21). Made of mirrors, it reflected the blue sky—the heavens—and prepared priests for work within the Holy Place. Before working, the priests washed their hands and feet. Their hands touched holy objects; their feet connected to the earth, which was polluted by the people's sins. Both hands and feet needed cleansing.

Once cleansed, a priest could go into the actual tent home. It was enclosed and covered with four layers: white linen covered with goat hair, ram skin, and an outer layer of a kind of leather. It wasn't impressive to see, but those who entered were in a noticeably different realm. They were moving from the earthly to the heavenly, the distance between heaven and earth being only the thickness of the curtain. Cherubim were sewn into the entrance. They evoked Eden and the angelic guards at the entrance.

Once inside, the first room was the Holy Place, where everything was gold in contrast to the less costly bronze that dominated the outer courtyard. In this room, light came only from a golden lampstand that was decorated as a living tree. It echoed the light on the first day of creation, and it was joined to the tree of life from the garden—light and life in contrast to darkness and death. The lampstand had seven lamps. The light of these lamps pointed toward a gold-covered table that had twelve loaves of bread (Ex. 25:30), which symbolized God's care for all twelve family groups within Israel. In other words, God's people were in the Holy Place. God's dwelling has always been intended for his people, and his light shines on them.

The altar of incense was the piece of furniture closest to the next curtain, which opened into the Most Holy Place. Like everything else in the tabernacle, the altar of incense was crammed with meaning and revealed an extravagant host. He had brought the beauty of himself and his home even to humanity's sense of smell. Yet there was more. The sacrifices offered about 50 feet away sent smoke into the heavens—the Holy Place *was* the heavens. Here, the altar's smoke became a sweet and pleasing aroma to the Lord. This smoke represented the prayers of the supplicants for forgiveness and fellowship, and those prayers were sweet and acceptable.[13]

Farthest into the tabernacle was the Most Holy Place. The Lord gave access to the Most Holy Place only once a year, and only to the High Priest. It was the throne room of God. In it was a golden box or ark that evoked the Lord's footstool. It contained a sample of manna and a copy of the Ten Commandments. These elements spoke clearly of God's kingly rule, his provision, and his personal speech. Two angels, facing each other, looked down on the ark of the covenant. Above them was the throne of God, invisible and real. This glory, sequestered for a time, was just waiting to bust loose.

God was present. This was "where I will meet with you, to speak to you" (Ex. 29:42). The tabernacle was a visual representation of God's world along with specific instruction on how his people were to come near. Each detail was intended to prepare humanity to recognize Jesus when he came and gathered all these details into himself.

Response

This blueprint makes the rest of Scripture much more understandable because there are so many references and allusions to it. Interpreted rightly, the tabernacle is both a home and a path. Being mapped out for you is the pathway to heaven. The house itself holds endless wonders. But it is humanity's movement farther in or farther away that deserves your attention. Review the blueprint and furniture, and see in them a path that leads farther in.

15

Priests Clothed

The tabernacle was the center of life in Israel. The Lord designed it, and the most skilled craftsmen carried out his directions. So it is surprising that *beauty* is first used to describe priests rather than the tabernacle itself. The words *glory* and *beauty*, when applied to mere human beings, are arresting. They announce that we can and will be rid of the disgrace that separates us from *his* beauty, and he himself will do it. In other words, he will supply garments that we can wear in his presence.

> Bring near to you Aaron your brother, and his sons with him, from among the people of Israel, to serve me as priests—Aaron and Aaron's sons, Nadab and Abihu, Eleazar and Ithamar. And you shall make holy garments for Aaron your brother, for glory and for beauty. (Ex. 28:1–2)

The way to this glory and beauty is to be clothed. That was always God's intent. Not nakedness but investiture. Not dead skins but priestly vestments. God has designed our clothes, and they will make us quite presentable.

Exodus 28 and 29 prescribe the garments for the high priest as well as the garments for all the other priests who served in the tabernacle. The high priest's garments received the most detail and was singled out as being beautiful. Even without knowing the symbolic details of the garment, we still know it was something special. Colorful yarns of gold, blue, and purple; the finest linen; a gold breastplate; and a turban suitable for a king. The linen and yarns were the same as those used for the tabernacle coverings.

Though we don't know exactly what the priests understood of this design, we do know that image bearers—human beings—were the ones intended to represent God most accurately. The tabernacle, indeed, reflected his glory, but walking, living tabernacles were always the plan. The priestly coverings pointed to the Spirit-filled tabernacles that were to come, when we would all be made holy in Jesus Christ.

God's people were represented throughout the garments. Shoulder pieces were inlaid with onyx stones, one on each shoulder, and engraved on these stones were the names of Israel's twelve tribes. Over the linen garments was a breastplate with twelve jewels, each inscribed with a tribe's name. In other words, the high priest carried the people everywhere, even into the Most Holy Place.

An inscrutable feature of this breastplate was the Urim and the Thummim. These seem to be two stones, perhaps in a pouch, that aided the priest in wise judgment. We don't know the details of how this happened, but something was coming into view. The image of God in humanity was being restored. The discernment and wisdom lost at Eden were available because God was with his people.

The final item mentioned is the turban. It has royal, crown-like overtones, but that isn't what stands out. What attracts our attention is the engraving. "You shall make a plate of pure gold and engrave on it, like the engraving of a signet, 'Holy to the LORD'" (Ex. 28:36).

When you take a step back, it becomes clear: the priestly garment mimicked the tabernacle. There was an undergarment of white linen, just like the curtains. The names of the people were rendered in the garment, just like the names were rendered in the bread found in the Holy Place. The headpiece identified the wearer as holy, as the tent was holy. And the woven colors with the metallic gold threads shimmered in the light. They evoked the fiery presence of God's glory. The priest was a living version of the tabernacle. The priest and tabernacle both imaged God.[14]

The mind reels. "A day in your courts is better than a thousand elsewhere" (Ps. 84:10). The priests were blessed to be attendants at God's residence, but their presence there pointed to a much greater reality: his presence with his people would be so intimate that he would actually reside within them.

In the beginning, the life-giving Spirit animated our earthly bodies, and he will do it again. We look ahead and see that we are, both singularly and corporately, living tabernacles, and a tabernacle is where God resides with his people. "Do you not know that your body is a temple of the Holy Spirit within you, whom you have from God?" (1 Cor. 6:19). The Father over us, Jesus with us, and the Spirit in us—all this intimacy is now in view in the priestly story.

Response

1. The priestly garments received alterations over time. Watch for fine linen. These were the simpler garments of the other priests and Levites, and they were associated with righteousness (Isa. 61:10; Rev. 19:8). They will eventually double as wedding garments, as we are finally and fully united to Jesus Christ. This is the way to life without hiding. Have you considered

that these priestly garments are your own? How would you live differently were you to recognize that you wear them?

2. The story of closeness to God moves ahead with small steps. The tabernacle and the priestly garments point to a more perfect union with God and other people, one in which God's people are portable tabernacles. Have you ever considered the moveable tabernacle as a variation of your God-given identity? How do you live as a tabernacle?

16

Job Descriptions

The heart of the priestly job description is fellowship with the Lord, enjoying his hospitality and protection, living in his house. May we never think that dour obedience is the essence of life in Christ. Lavish meals, satisfaction, peace, and pleasure are the lot of God's priests. It could be no other way when we are invited to live at the junction of heaven and earth. Yet life is busy at this meeting place. There is much to do. Our identity as priests is accompanied by a meaningful mission. Boredom is not an option.

For the early priests, there were the weak, the orphaned, the widows, and the poor to care for and to encourage others to do the same—to lend with an open hand, to be generous as we have been shown generosity (Deut. 15:1–18). There were also wars and conflicts, and people had to be prepared for battle:

> When you draw near to the battle, the priest shall come forward and speak to the people and say to them, "Hear, O Israel, today you are drawing near for battle against your enemies: let not your heart faint. Do not fear or panic or

be in dread of them, for the LORD your God is he who goes with you to fight for you against your enemies to give you the victory." (Deut. 20:2–4)

These early descriptions of the priestly mission were always pointing toward something more and some*one* more. The mission converges on Jesus, the true high priest, and from him our job description explodes with new meaning. For example, we still care for the poor, needy, and burdened, but with maturity comes an awareness that we too are poor and needy (2 Cor. 12:1–10), and our care for others becomes infused with compassion (Heb. 5:1–3). Likewise, we continue to be warriors who encourage other warriors, but now we see the real enemy and his most lethal strategies (Eph. 6:10–18). So we turn toward our primary fight. We stand firm against anything in us that harbors satanic sympathies. We wage war against our own self-serving desires (notice how they inevitably splinter relationships and mimic Satan's murderous ways), and we help each other in that fight. These details are seen in three different aspects of the priests' job description. Each expresses our identity and purpose, and each can be expressed with infinite variety.

Fill the earth with wise, discerning royal priests. This filling is a global component of the job description. It began, "Be fruitful and multiply and fill the earth and subdue it" (Gen. 1:28). God had unfurled a canvas, and human beings were the painters commissioned to develop it. It left much to creativity and imagination.

As with the rest of God's animate creation, such as plants and animals, people were to populate the earth. We are priestly offspring, and we hope for a much larger family. The God who gives life gives us the potential to imitate him by giving life. We do this by having children. But what sets us apart from the subhuman kingdom is that we can invite children to follow Jesus and be instructed into life at its fullest, and we can invite the world to be born into a new family. Jesus commissioned us in a way that captured the true meaning of this original mandate:

> Go therefore and make disciples of all nations, baptizing them in the name of the Father and of the Son and of the Holy Spirit, teaching them to observe all that I have commanded you. (Matt. 28:19–20)

The job of subduing the earth continues unabated from the original commission. We are stewards of earth. But the souls of humanity have become our primary stewardship. Our aim is for baptisms, which indicates God's cleansing of us, but, even more, baptism means that we identify with and belong to him. We have been brought back into his family, and in this family, we grow in Christ, teach about Christ, and discern what is right and good.

Samuel was clear about this aspect of the priestly job, even when the people he served rebelled against the Lord:

> As for me, far be it from me that I should sin against the LORD by ceasing to pray for you, and I will instruct you in the good and the right way (1 Sam. 12:23; cf. Deut. 33:10).

Priests call children, neighbors, and the world to draw near to Jesus.

Care for the peace and purity of the believing community. Such caring is a localized aspect of our priestly commission. The job of priests is to protect and keep God's house. When Adam and Eve failed in the original testing grounds of Eden, God designated cherubim to protect his sanctuary. In the next phase of redemptive history, cherubim gave way to priests. Humans were being restored. The priests were the ones who kept guard (Num. 18:3–4; Deut. 18:7). They were given a substantial manual with precise direction. There was to be very little ad-libbing. Instead, they were trained at discerning the ways of God. Yet even with this detailed direction, priests failed and ran headlong into the idolatries that they were commissioned to guard against.

As it turned out, their failure was written into the manual. The blood of animals pointed to the need for a better sacrifice, and the human heart's instinctive bent toward independence pointed toward the need for a new heart, not just a rehabilitated one. Only when Jesus became the high priest and sacrifice and tabernacle did the royal priesthood become the church. Yet the church, too, has its struggles. We have divisions, false teachers, and sinfully favored preachers as well as all the other sins known to humanity.

The apostle Paul protected the peace and purity of the churches with great zeal:

> Do you not know that you are God's temple and that God's Spirit dwells in you? If anyone destroys God's temple, God will destroy him. For God's temple is holy, and you are that temple. (1 Cor. 3:16–17)

In this passage, he uses the image of the *church* as temple rather than the individual as temple, and he guards the church by protesting the cult of personality and favoritism in the church. When he wrote about the Lord's Supper, he turned his attention to distinctions between rich and poor where the rich received preferred treatment. This could not be in God's temple, he wrote. Tensions and division were to be reconciled before the priestly meal (1 Cor. 11:17–33). Then his pastoral letter shifted images from the church as God's temple to the church as body of Christ (1 Cor. 12:12–30), which is even more intimate than tabernacle language.

For us, this means that we are vigilant about any hints of favoritism or strained relationships, first in our own hearts and relationships, then in others.

- Do we pursue some people in our church but not others?
- Do we avoid those who are different from us?
- Does anyone have something against us?
- Have we gossiped about others in the church?

These questions are not simply our attempts to do the right thing. They are features of our priestly humanity, and our attentiveness to them is our purpose and calling.

Reflect the Lord (Ex. 34:33; Ps. 34:5). A more personal way to envision this aspect of the priestly job description is to think of Moses, who reflected God's greatness and holiness. Moses wanted above all else to witness the glory of God. As the Lord came close, he revealed a part of his glory to Moses. Moses, in turn, literally reflected the brightness of God. As God is light, so Moses reflected that light:

> When Moses came down from Mount Sinai, with the two tablets of the testimony in his hand as he came down from the mountain, Moses did not know that the skin of his face shone because he had been talking with God. Aaron and all the people of Israel saw Moses, and behold, the skin of his face shone, and they were afraid to come near him. (Ex. 34:29–30)

This story is unparalleled in the Old Testament. Only here do we witness someone's countenance change because he or she was close to the Lord. It is, however, a priestly story. Moses represented the people and was invited to draw near. When he drew near, he took on a characteristic of the one he beheld. Garments can reflect the Lord; faces, too, can reflect him. (More on this later.) The story will be picked up again in the New Testament, and it will be even better (2 Cor. 3:12–18).

Response

1. Use your own words to describe the three aspects of the priestly job description.

2. Identify an application of each aspect of the priest's job description.

17

Priests at Work

Since priests predated kings and prophets, some of the duties that subsequently fell to kings and prophets were originally performed by the priests. Responsibility for these duties was determined by lot. Some priests inspected houses for mildew; others examined skin diseases. Some taught the law and judged in disputes. Priests are best known, however, for their work in the tabernacle and the later temple built under Solomon. They had to adhere to strict laws of cleanliness, as did their family. They could have no obvious physical defects or abnormalities. Their Levite coworkers, who maintained the tabernacle, were called into service between the ages of thirty and fifty (Num. 4:47), in keeping with the physicality of the work. There seemed to be no age restrictions on the priests, who served as they were able until their death.

Sanctified

Before they began their ministry, priests had to be set apart (i.e., sanctified or made holy). This separation was apparent long before their ordination ceremony, even when they were lounging at home.

Perhaps the most coveted blessing for the ancient Hebrew was land, yet the priests received no land. Families depended on their land, and it was meant to bless the generations that followed as well. For the priests and Levites, God set apart cities. Instead of making their living from the land, the priests were given portions of certain sacrifices, some that were eaten in the tabernacle and some that were given to the priest's family, and they received income from the tithes, offerings, and "devoted things" brought by the people (Num. 18:14, 24).

The "devoted things" consisted mostly of firstborn and first fruits. These were uniquely the Lord's, and the people brought either their first and best to the tabernacle or a predetermined cash-value for its place. What the people gave to the Lord, the Lord shared with the priests and the Levites. So when Scripture identified the blessings of land and inheritance, the priests could think about their more prized inheritance:

> And the LORD said to Aaron, "You shall have no inheritance in their land, neither shall you have any portion among them. I am your portion and your inheritance among the people of Israel." (Num. 18:20)

People are more important than things—that is a good general rule. But the Lord's promise to Aaron is something even greater. Look for it up ahead when Jesus says, "Fear not, little flock, for it is your Father's good pleasure to give you the kingdom" (Luke 12:32). When you get the Lord, you get everything else thrown in. The only challenge is that the early priests and we ourselves have received an inheritance that is largely unseen. But even here, we are aided each day by signs and symbols that have been designed by God, that reflect his character, and that anticipate the fulfillment of his promises. Moses, Aaron, and the Israelites had the tabernacle. We have baptism, the Lord's Supper, and the Spirit, who opens our eyes to the unseen.

Priests were set apart for their work in a formal ceremony. The process was called "ordination" or "consecration" (see figure 5 on p. 72). They were already "clean," but they also had to be made holy. The ceremony began as the priests-to-be washed, dressed with the wardrobe that God designed, and were anointed with oil (Ex. 29:7; Lev. 8:10–12). Anointing oil later appears in the installations of Israel's kings, healing for the sick, and treatment of honored guests. *Messiah* means "anointed one." In this case, anointing means that God set apart the man for special purposes.

Next came sacrifices, which began with a sin offering that was prescribed for specific sins. A priest first laid hands on a sacrificial animal as a way of identifying with a substitute that would die in his place. He would kill the animal, and its blood was placed at the base of the altar, the sides, and the horns or vertical protrusions at the four corners. The base of the altar met the earth, the side of the altar represented the tabernacle itself, and the horns were its highest point, closest to the heavens. In other words, the sacrificial area itself had to be sanctified.

The sin offering was followed by a burnt offering, which seems to have general uncleanness in view. The sacrificial animal was wholly consumed on the altar. No part was used for any other purpose. No blood was taken from it. Here we are told that this sacrifice was a pleasing aroma to the Lord.

The next sacrifice was unique to the priestly consecration and was called the "ordination offering" (Lev. 8:22). It began like the sin offering. A priest first laid his hands on the animal, and then it was slain. Here in the ordination offering, the blood was placed not on the tabernacle but on the priest himself. Since priests were a kind of mobile tabernacle, the blood was placed on the big toe of the right foot, the thumb of the right hand, and the earlobes—the point where priests touch the earth, the means of service in the tabernacle, and the place on the body closest to the heavens. An offering of bread was then introduced to the sacrifice. It essentially said, what we have is from the Lord, and we devote it to the Lord. This offering was consummated with a meal in which the priest enjoyed God's hospitality at the entrance of the tabernacle.

The ordination service was for the male offspring of Aaron, but we know where the story is going. All God's people were soon to be included in this ordination process. The details of the service look different for us because all these sacrifices have been condensed into the work of Jesus. But the rhythm of life for the Aaronic priesthood continues to be the rhythm of our lives. Priests were:

- cleansed from sin
- devoted to the Lord
- thankful for the Lord's provision
- blessed by his fellowship and care

Sacrifices

By the time of King Solomon the tabernacle was given a more permanent place in Jerusalem, and there were thousands of priests and Levites. They were clustered into divisions, each having its specialties: administration, bakers for the bread of the presence, those who checked scales for fair transactions, gatekeepers, musicians, singers, and the priests who oversaw the sacrificial system itself.

When a priest was on duty at the altar, his morning began with a few domestic tasks. There was an offering on the altar that had been burning all night. Its ashes had to be disposed of outside the tabernacle, and the fire had to be stoked. Meanwhile, he was reminded that the smoke had been going up before the Lord, as a pleasing aroma, for the entire night. Even while the people slept, the Lord was actively making a way for his presence to remain in the camp.

The entrance was opened for the morning service around nine o'clock (Ex. 29:38–46; Num. 28:1–8). A priest sounded the trumpet (1 Chron. 16:6). Another priest entered the holy place, trimmed the candles, and burned incense. In the courtyard other priests presented a burnt offering to the Lord along with food and drink offerings. The service closed with a benediction spoken over the community.

Throughout the day, the people came to offer various sacrifices and offerings. To make an animal sacrifice, the worshiper laid hands on the animal and killed it near the entrance of the tabernacle. Everything was up close, participatory, and personal. Once the animal was sacrificed, the priests took over.

There were about eight different kinds of sacrifices, which can be loosely organized around the burnt offering and the peace offering. The burnt offering, along with the sin and guilt offering, always included the blood of animals. These offerings were for forgiveness of sin and purification, and they were expressions of devotion to God. The peace offering, along with cereal, drink, grain, vow, freewill, and wave offerings, was also an expression of personal devotion but these offerings especially communicated reconciliation and fellowship with the Lord.

In the evening, around four o'clock, the morning service was repeated.

All of this created a pleasing aroma to the Lord, and it was God's plan for meeting with his people (Ex. 29:42–43). Did the sacrifices earn God's favor? No, they were in recognition of what God had done and would do, and they were effective because of his mercy. And the daily rhythm was gradually inculcated into the hearts of the priests and the people. The people were:

- cleansed from sin
- devoted to the Lord
- thankful for the Lord's provision
- blessed by his fellowship and care

The Lord would assure the people of these things again the next day.

Holy Days

There were other rhythms too. Some days were common, some were holy. We can identify many of those holy days by noting cycles of seven:

- The Sabbath is the seventh day of the week.
- The Day of Atonement is in the seventh month.
- The year for releasing debts is the seventh or sabbatical year.
- The Year of Jubilee is after the forty-ninth year, or seven times seven. (Deut. 25:8–17)

Other holy days filled in the gaps. Keep track of three feasts or festival periods in particular, when able-bodied people celebrated with a trip to the temple in Jerusalem. These appear frequently in the New Testament.

The first festival. The year began with the Passover and went immediately into a seven-day harvest celebration that included the Feast of Unleavened Bread and the Feast of Firstfruits (Lev. 23:4–14).

The second festival. Seven weeks and a day later was another harvest festival, the Feast of Weeks, which was later known as Pentecost.

The third festival. The seventh month was sanctified at the very beginning with the Feast of Trumpets as preparation for the Day of Atonement, which came ten days later. On the fifteenth day of the same month was the Feast of Booths, lasting an entire week.

All of these were marked by special sacrifices, rest for the people, and particular remembrances. But the weekly Sabbath was the true pulse of the community's spiritual life.

The Sabbath. On the Sabbath, priests were busy with double the morning sacrifices; the bread in the Holy Place was replaced with freshly baked bread (Num. 28:9–10), and more worshipers gathered. They were rehearsing a story that went back to the beginning.

The first verse of Genesis has seven words, as if to keep us moving through the days of creation until we get to day seven. We have a vested interest in day six, and the creation of humanity stands out among the first six days, but the Sabbath is where we want to go. On the Sabbath God rested, and he invites us to rest with him. This is not so much that everyone takes a nap on the Sabbath. The point is that we don't have to work, so we have time to meet with the Lord—and he meets with us. The point is *shalom* or peace, not sleep. Perhaps those walks with God in the garden were Sabbath walks, when nothing else needed to be done. Only the Sabbath is identified as holy in the creation story.

Imagine the impact on those who first heard of the Sabbath. They had just come out of slavery, where one day was the same as the next. The people worked. There was nothing else. Now a day was set apart for the people to rest in God. With the Sabbath, God essentially proclaimed that his people were not slaves but a royal priesthood.

Worship at the tabernacle, a different pace to the day, the notable absence of labor, more purposeful conversations (Isa. 58:13), reflection on God's mighty acts, joy at being invited into what is his, participation with God in what he called "my Sabbaths" (Ex. 31:13)—these are some of the ways that God instructed people to fill this holy day. All of it was an expression of trust in the Lord who provides.

But fears can creep in. The first discussion of the Sabbath and its practices concerned the gathering of manna (Ex. 16:22–30). The people were told to collect extra manna on the day before the Sabbath so that they would not have to gather any on the following day. This meant that they were to trust in the Lord's care for them more than in the work of their hands. Trust is essential to a relationship. Without it, there are merely parallel lives and relationships of convenience. The Sabbath was an opportunity to trust the Lord—to give up a sense of personal control—and the people failed.

Imagine harvesttime. With crops at their peak, and with the Sabbath, a day of harvesting was lost. The Sabbath was a good test for the soul. Trust does not come naturally; self-interest does. The Sabbath was an opportunity to say that all things come from the Lord. It was also how God's people were distinguished from their neighbors. Israel was the nation that rested with their God one day each week, and since he is over the entire earth and everything that fills it, he could be trusted to care for their needs.

Looking ahead to Jesus, the Sabbath remained central to Hebrew practices, but the holy day was in danger of becoming a burden because the leaders had added so many laws to Sabbath observance. This is the context for Jesus's well-known words, "Come to me, all who labor and are heavy laden, and I will give you rest" (Matt. 11:28). Here Jesus reclaims the Sabbath and, in a blatant admission that he is God, he calls people to find their rest in him.

In the Gospels, "on the Sabbath" is a marker that something important is about to happen. Jesus had come close, life was breaking in, heaven was piercing earth, and death was being pushed aside. Withered hands were being healed. Disciples were being fed. The Sabbath was a time for blessing, not burdens. All the human laws had made the day about personal achievement and self-righteousness rather than trust and rest. If it were otherwise, perhaps the leaders would have recognized the Lord of glory and worshiped him. Instead, they sought to catch Jesus breaking their version of the Sabbath, and it was because of Jesus's acts on the Sabbath that they sought to kill him (John 5:18).

After the resurrection, the early church began to meet on the first day of the week, and Sunday gradually became the Christian version of the Sabbath (Acts 20:7; 1 Cor. 16:1–2). Since the Holy Spirit had come to dwell in the people of God, every day was sanctified, as the believers met daily for worship, prayer, and study of Scripture. But the Sabbath is set apart, so we set apart time to rest from our physical burdens and to remember that Jesus himself has taken on our spiritual burdens. The Sabbath reminds us that rest and peace can only be found in the Lord of the Sabbath.

The Day of Atonement. The Sabbath dominated the weekly calendar. The Sabbath of Sabbaths (Lev. 16:31), or Day of Atonement, dominated the yearly calendar. It was the only day when the curtain to the Most Holy Place was lifted for one representative of the people.

Scripture gives this day, the Day of Atonement, a curious introduction through the story of Nadab and Abihu (Lev. 10:1–2). These sons of Aaron chose to go farther into God's tent when neither was the high priest, and they attempted this with "unauthorized fire," which may have been coals that were not from the altar. God's judgment was immediate. The fire of God consumed them. The judgment was so apt that Aaron and two other sons who were also serving in the tabernacle were not permitted to grieve. The fire of God will either ignite the pleasing aroma of incense before his throne or consume those who are indifferent to his clear commands. Given how this story precedes the instructions for the Day of Atonement, we can understand why the day was approached soberly and with fasting rather than feasting.

The necessary elements for this day were a bull and a ram for the high priest and two goats for the people. The high priest began by bringing a young bull and a ram—his own animals—for a sin offering and burnt offering for himself and his family. Having bathed completely, and wearing a simple tunic, he took coals from the altar, incense, and sacrificial blood, and he went behind the last curtain, into the Most Holy Place.

When the incense was placed on the coals, it created a cloud. This both symbolized the heavens and concealed the ark from clear sight, which was a form of protection for the priest. He then sprinkled the blood on the seat of the ark, which represented the footstool of God. The blood was for the cleansing and removal of the high priest's sin and that of his household.

When he came out of the tent, he took one of the goats, sacrificed it, and followed the same steps for the people as he did for his own household. Then he took the live goat, pressed his hands on the goat's head, and confessed the sins and rebellion of the people, symbolically transferring those sins to the goat. The goat was then led into the wilderness where it was released. Having been identified with the people, the goat was excluded and sent away, far from the presence of the Lord into a lifeless place. After final sacrifices and final washings for the high priest, the day that the Lord prescribed was complete, and the people were assured, "You shall be clean before the LORD from all your sins" (Lev. 16:30).

So many spiritual realities were crammed into this day. Sin was purged by a substitute acceptable to the Lord, blood was sprinkled to bring life to people who had been polluted, and the wandering goat took sins "as far as the east is from the west" as a way to illustrate how far God removes his people from their sins (Ps. 103:12). God was making a way to get closer. To use Genesis language, a new Adam could go past the cherubim that guarded the presence of God. The Day of Atonement assured the people that intimacy with the Lord was still the plan, but it would happen gradually.

As we bring these holy days into the present, what is most obvious is that our sins are our deepest and most profound problem. Our struggles with money, broken relationships, and poor health will be over when we see Jesus, but our sins have eternal implications unless they are sprinkled with the cleansing blood of the Lamb.

Priests knew this, or at least they had every opportunity to know it. Apart from such knowledge, the sacrificial system would have been nothing more than a strange pageant, and, later, Jesus's death would be merely an expression of service to others that we should imitate. All modern-day priests, therefore, should be able to identify personal sins. We could put this more strongly: to be fully human is to know our sins, to know that the sacrifice of Jesus has taken our sins away from the presence of God, and to do battle against ongoing temptations. This immediately raises questions:

> What sins have you seen in your own heart in the last day? Have you confessed them to the Lord and, if appropriate, to those whom you sinned against?
>
> If you have desires that you love more than Jesus, have you asked for help?
>
> Do you rest in how the blood of Christ has both covered your sins and removed them from the presence of God, as if your sins are removed "as far as the east is from the west" (Ps. 103:12)?
>
> Do you have zeal to fight sin as part of God's blessing to you?

Blessing

The priestly story is that of God reclaiming us, bringing us close, and blessing us. The Lord is not under compulsion to show us this kindness. He blesses us because it is his nature. He is inclined to bless, he has made a way to deal with sin so he can bless, and we certainly need his blessing. In the Old Testament God's blessing extended to health, care for family, sufficient food, land, and protection from enemies. In the New Testament, the blessing is that we have been brought into Jesus himself. We have been brought even closer.

To bless is to show favor, and to be blessed is to experience the happiness of such favor. When we bless someone, we want our pleasure in that person to be obvious, and we want the very best for that person. When God blesses us, he makes public his pleasure in us and assures us that his intent is to give us the best of things. God himself pronounced blessing on Adam and Eve (Gen. 1:28), and Jesus continued this tradition (Matt. 5:1–12).

And there is more. When God speaks words over his creation, his creative power is put to work. Life appears. This happens with the earth, the sky, the seas, and with us. Blessing is God's procreative power being brought to our lives. It is necessary for us if we are to live as he intends. Jesus said, "The thief comes only to steal and kill and destroy. I came that they may have life and have it abundantly" (John 10:10).

As people who have been blessed, he also invites us to partner with him and speak his blessing on others. This public blessing was a privilege and responsibility of the priests at the close of each day's sacrifices. The inaugural blessing, which marked the opening of the tabernacle, was particularly spectacular:

> Moses and Aaron went into the tent of meeting, and when they came out they blessed the people, and the glory of the

L<small>ORD</small> appeared to all the people. And fire came out from before the L<small>ORD</small> and consumed the burnt offering and the pieces of fat on the altar, and when all the people saw it, they shouted and fell on their faces. (Lev. 9:23–24)

The blessing was the occasion for the glory of the Lord to be briefly unleashed. As with Elijah, the Lord sent fire from heaven that consumed the offering that had been laid on the altar, the aroma was undoubtedly sweet, and the people worshiped him.

Here is true humanity on display: the Lord blesses his people, and they bless or worship him in return. Worship can take the form of falling on our face, singing, or taking small steps of obedience and love in his name. Whatever form it takes, worship is humanity at its most dignified and beautiful.

Then the priests settled into their daily rhythms of public blessing:

The L<small>ORD</small> spoke to Moses, saying, "Speak to Aaron and his sons, saying, Thus you shall bless the people of Israel: you shall say to them,

The L<small>ORD</small> bless you and keep you;
The L<small>ORD</small> make his face to shine upon you and be gracious to you;
The L<small>ORD</small> lift up his countenance upon you and give you peace.
"So shall they put my name upon the people of Israel, and I will bless them." (Num. 6:22–27)

The blessing picks up momentum through three phrases. The original Hebrew begins with a three-word blessing: "The L<small>ORD</small> bless and keep you"; then a five-word blessing; then a seven-word blessing. Each adds more richness to the blessing.

"The L<small>ORD</small> bless you and keep you." Psalm 121 expands on this entrance to the priestly blessing. "The Lord is your

keeper" (v. 5). He is close enough to shade you from the sun, always awake, and protecting your very life.

"*The* L'ORD *make his face to shine upon you and be gracious to you.*" Psalm 80 attaches to this stanza and turns it into a refrain: "Restore us, O God; let your face shine, that we may be saved" (vv. 3, 7, 19). The lampstand is in view as well as the light that is characteristic of his presence. The blessing is that you would know his rescue when you are overwhelmed.

"*The* L'ORD *lift up his countenance upon you and give you peace.*" The final blessing is most personal. The Lord tells you that he sees and hears you. The face of the Father is toward his children. By his gentle care he will make things right and give deep and lasting peace.

The priests probably spoke this particular succinct and warm blessing as part of the tabernacle worship, as do many pastors today. You, too, can speak these words over others, and you are at liberty to embellish them and personalize them. But you must bless others in the name of Jesus. This is a premiere feature of your work.

Response

1. There is much here. All of it is about how we can draw near to the Lord. What seems especially important?

2. How would you describe the rhythms of life, and how do they guide your life?

18

"Be Holy as I Am Holy"

Holy is first about God and how everything about him is holy. His love is holy; his justice is holy. God's love and justice are different from anything we have known on earth, but they don't put him in a quarantined bubble. The refrain in his house is, "Holy, holy, holy is the LORD of hosts; the whole earth is full of his glory" (Isa. 6:3). His holiness expands. He goes farther and farther out, reaches into human uncleanness, and gathers people into his holiness. That is his pleasure. This holiness or set-apartness is shared with us so we are made holy. It is a status that the Lord bestows on us. Then, with that change in status, we *change*. We practice and *grow* in holiness, which brings with it a greater intensity of closeness.

> For I am the LORD your God. Consecrate yourselves therefore, and be holy, for I am holy. (Lev. 11:44; also 19:2)

> So you shall remember and do all my commandments, and be holy to your God. (Num. 15:40)

Simply put, the way of holiness is obedience. This obedience is our personal response to him. It is the devotion that was expressed through the burnt offering and other sacrifices. Though obedience can feel almost painful at times, such as when we take a stand against sinful temptations, obedience is good. It is one way we move from being merely human and enslaved to our desires to being fully human and more alive.

Obedience, however, is a means to an end. Obedience serves the purpose of our communion with him. This goal of communion is clear from God's presence in the garden (Gen. 3:8); from Jesus's prayer, "I in them and you in me" (John 17:23); and from our marital consummation when Jesus returns (Rev. 21:1–2). Fellowship bound up with worship, praise, and downright enjoyment is what we are after.

Try this. Instead of considering your growth in Christ as progressive sanctification, which is a fine expression identifying that growth in holiness does not come all at once, and seems quite slow at times, think of it as "progressive nearness."[15] Sin separates, even after we are made holy. When we turn from sin, we turn back to the light and life, and we experience fellowship with a clear conscience. God's laws are instructions about how to be in relationship with him. This is reflected in all our human relationships as there are rules in a relationship that, when followed, protect the relationship and move it toward greater intimacy.

This fellowship with the Lord is basic to our proclaiming "the excellencies of him who called you out of darkness into his marvelous light" (1 Pet. 2:9). The picture here is not so much that we have been in a dark prison and can finally come out into the sun and fresh air. It is that we have made choices that have led us into solitary confinement, and we live with an abiding sense of personal alienation from everything good. Into this disaster comes the Holy God, who is the light. He invites us to come to him and warms and comforts us in his presence. Somehow, through his Spirit, we actually become "partakers of the divine nature" (2 Pet. 2:4), which is very close. Progressive nearness makes this growth and change increasingly beautiful, satisfying, and attractive.

Response

1. Obedience serves the purpose of being near. When you violate wedding vows, you move away from your spouse. Priests, of all people, should be able to see the relational goals in their obedience. How do relational goals make obedience to Christ more attractive?

2. *Holy* identifies both God and us. How would you describe it?

19

In God's Courtroom

As priests, we are consecrated by God and made holy; then we grow in holiness. We are brought into Christ and become partners in his righteous ways. Yet our imperfections are always before us. Sin remains a part of us in such a way that, in ourselves, we are always dirty. This, it seems, creates a problem. It is not good to be sinners in his presence.

The Hebrew priests give us some encouragement. They were officially clean and could work in the Lord's house, but none was perfect, none was fully devoted to the Lord or innocent in thought, word, and deed. No priest ever rested in his own perfections. He rested in God's mercy and the confidence that the one who invites less-than-clean people to live with him is the one who figures out how that will happen. A vision given to Zechariah gives more detail.

Zechariah received seven visions. The fourth and key vision concerns a high priest named Joshua. His specific identity is unimportant because *we* are Joshua.

The scene is the heavenly court. There were times when spiritual beings assembled before the Lord. The initial occurrence was in the garden, in which Satan's appearance may have been part of that tradition. The next mention of this assembly is in Job, though no humans were among them. In Zechariah 3 we are taken into the heavenly court again. Those identified are Joshua, Zechariah, Satan, and the angel of the Lord, who is Jesus.

> Then he showed me Joshua the high priest standing before the angel of the LORD, and Satan standing at his right hand to accuse him. And the LORD said to Satan, "The LORD rebuke you, O Satan! The LORD who has chosen Jerusalem rebuke you! Is not this a brand plucked from the fire?" Now Joshua was standing before the angel, clothed with filthy garments. And the angel said to those who were standing before him, "Remove the filthy garments from him." And to him he said, "Behold, I have taken your iniquity away from you, and I will clothe you with pure vestments." (Zech. 3:1–4)

It is all too familiar. Satan brings his accusations. How can the Lord allow a defiled people to draw near to the Lord? How can God love people like us? Satan is the prosecutor who makes his case. The case would seem to have promise because the people had been unfaithful to the Lord and have reason to believe that the verdict will be "not my people" (Hos. 1:9).

The Lord's response is swift and clear. The *accuser* is the one judged. "The LORD rebuke you"(Zech. 3:2). The Lord had, in fact, sent his people away because they were committed to turning away, but his intent had always been to protect them from his consuming fire. He had made promises to Abraham that he would keep in Jesus. But these realities can seem far away when the court is in session.

After Satan's rebuke, the angel of the Lord turns to Joshua— to us. We have seen this before in the garden, so we might expect that we would be next in line for judgment. In Genesis, the Lord first spoke of the serpent's judgment, and then he turned to Eve and Adam. But the judge reveals that he is not only a judge. He is also the advocate who comes to our defense. Even more, he is our advocate-defender-sacrifice-beautifier who will take upon himself the burden of qualifying his people to be with him.

While we stand there in filthy garments, heavenly attendants remove those rags, and we are redressed with laundered, priestly vestments. All eyes are on Jesus. He does all this himself. We witness his work. When the priests went daily to the basin of the tabernacle for cleansing, the water pointed to what was to happen in this divine courtroom. For *his* namesake, not because of our inherent worth or capacity, he forgives and cleanses us.

All this is so attractive and inviting that Zechariah can't help but say something. "I said, 'Let them put a clean turban on his head'" (v. 5). He wanted to see the completed outfit, which included the turban with its gold plaque inscribed, "Holy to the LORD" (see Ex. 28:36). In Zechariah's vision, the plaque is represented as a kingly signet stone with "Holy to the LORD" as its implied meaning.[16] It is upon this stone, which Jesus himself placed on us, that he directs his gaze and makes us recipients of his favor.[17]

In this vision the character of the Lord is on fuller display. He is not torn between loving people and consuming them in his anger. Instead, he has determined that we be with him, and he is always inclined to wash and forgive those who turn to him. Following Zechariah's lead, we are emboldened to come near. So we heed the call from the Lord that precedes this vision, "Return from your evil ways" (Zech. 1:4). When we are tempted to think that we are too dirty to return, we are reminded that he launders our clothes. That was never our job. And he delights to do it. Shame is no reason to turn away.

Yet we are witnessing something even deeper. This beautifying means that we begin to look more and more like God himself as we are being refashioned into his image. Communion is best when we share a likeness. We are becoming truly human, remade in the image of our Father and Creator. More still, "what the divine Angel is seen doing for Joshua in the vision, he would later do as the incarnate Servant-Son."[18] Jesus is the royal Branch mentioned at the end of Zechariah's vision. When he comes, he "will remove the iniquity of this land in a single day" (3:9), and everything will change. "In that day, declares the LORD of hosts, every one of you will invite his neighbor to come under his vine and under his fig tree" (3:10). In Jesus we know holiness and peace.

Response

1. When do you need to accuse your accuser? When are Satan's accusations against you especially effective, and how can you turn the tables and accuse him? The signet stone might help.

2. Isaiah 61:10 gives us an apt response. You might have read this before, but each successive reading will become richer and fuller. The priestly garments reflect the glory of God and are evidence that he will rescue his people. They are the same garments that will later be used for a wedding in which God and his people will be thoroughly united.

> I will greatly rejoice in the LORD;
> > my soul shall exult in my God,
> for he has clothed me with the garments of salvation;
> > he has covered me with the robe of righteousness,
> as a bridegroom decks himself like a priest with a
> > beautiful headdress,
> > and as a bride adorns herself with her jewels.
> > (Isa. 61:10)

20

A Tumultuous Interlude

The fortunes of the priests and the temple were bound together. As one went, so went the other. The priests rarely got it right. Once Israel settled in Canaan, they had an enduring tolerance for idolatry, so we shouldn't be surprised that the temple had its problems. At one point the Philistines took the ark of the covenant, which was the prized centerpiece of God's house.

The priests' influence grew, however, when Solomon completed the magnificent temple in Jerusalem (1 Kings 6–7; 2 Chron. 2–7). The dimensions of this temple were more than double those of the original tabernacle. Gold was everywhere, the number of workers multiplied, and the worship included processions of dancers, musicians, and singers. The psalms began to receive their present shape as King David became the prominent lyricist for temple worship. His psalms were intended for the morning and evening services, and they are best read with the temple in view. Everything was exquisite, at least on the outside. But the account in the book of Kings suggests that all was not well:

Solomon spent more time and expense on his own house than he did on the Lord's.

Solomon had a foreigner oversee the work, and this foreigner was paid with Israelite cities.

Solomon forced Hebrews into labor, which sounds peculiarly like the old Egyptian overlords.

Solomon took liberties with furniture dimensions and materials, which bent the tabernacle toward the pagan temples of that day.[19]

If you look closely, the story tends toward entropy. God's presence is less intense, less concentrated. The glory and presence of the Lord rested on the new temple (1 Kings 8:10–11; 2 Chron. 7:1–3), but idol worship, tacitly approved by Solomon, was followed by civil war and a divided kingdom. A long line of corrupt kings and idolatrous priests weakened Israel until the northern kingdom of Israel was destroyed by Assyria, and those tribes were not heard from again. Meanwhile the southern kingdom, the home of Jerusalem and the temple, was eventually sacked and destroyed by the Babylonians in 586 BC. This destruction was a great national tragedy, but it was spiritually anticlimactic. Ezekiel had already predicted these events, deportation of the people into exile had begun, and Ezekiel had witnessed the glory and presence of God already departed from the temple (Ezek. 10:18). When the Babylonians entered the Most Holy Place, there was no cloud of the presence, and the presence of God would not inhabit the Jerusalem temple again.

About fifty years later, when Persia routed Babylon, the Lord moved Cyrus, king of Persia, to send many exiles back to Jerusalem in order to rebuild the temple. With overtones of the exodus from Egypt, he sent them with the items that

Nebuchadnezzar of Babylon had plundered from the temple, and neighbors became generous in their gifts to the returning exiles.

The work on the second temple had begun. Rebuilding under Zerubbabel went well at first, but opposition from residents led to a court order to stop construction (Ezra 1–4). Ten years later, through the prophet Haggai's urging, the work was completed. Ezra and Nehemiah would soon return to give further leadership and complete the walls of the city.

It was becoming obvious that independence in that region of the world was hard to achieve. Israel existed on a critical trading route that connected three continents. As a result, nations vied for control, which would pay off as a steady stream of taxes and other revenue.

The Persian Empire gave way to Alexander the Great, whose early death left his generals scrambling for power. Two of those generals—Ptolemy to the south in Egypt and Seleucus to the north in Syria—contested the middle ground of Palestine for decades until the Seleucid king Antiochus Epiphanes took control of Jerusalem (168 BC). He appointed priesthoods to the highest bidders, and in a fit of pique over Roman encroachment, he took out his anger against Jerusalem by tearing down its walls, slaughtering residents, bringing prostitutes into the temple, and finally claiming the temple for Zeus and sacrificing pigs on the altar. This arguably was worse than the destruction of the temple by Babylon and is often identified as "the abomination that makes desolate" (Dan. 12:11). Many Jews tolerated these changes.

Some, however, stood firm. Mattathias, an Hasmonian or descendant of Asmoneus, began a revolt that continued with his sons. His sons were known by the name Maccabee, or "hammer." Through a number of battles, and with occasional assistance from other countries, Judah Maccabee captured

Jerusalem and reconsecrated the temple (164 BC), an event commemorated in the celebration of Hanukkah.

Later, Hasmoneans forged treaties and paid tribute to neighboring countries while also maintaining some political and religious power. They eventually combined the roles of high priest and regional king, which didn't sit well with some of the people. This is when the Pharisees and Sadducees began to appear as political rivals, with the Pharisees considering themselves to be the true keepers of the Hebrew traditions. The Pharisees were offended by this dual role of king and high priest and lobbied for separate roles. The two parties eventually led to a divided leadership, and the ensuing civil war introduced a clever advisor named Antipater.

Antipater was an Idumean who had been forced to convert to Judaism when his region was annexed to the Hasmonean kingdom, and he had worked himself into a position of power. Idumea was the name of the biblical Edom, which can be traced back to Esau. So, given the prophesied tensions between Esau and Jacob, we expect that things might not go well (Gen. 27:39–40).

Antipater's son, Herod the Great, was a more ruthless version of his father. He took a second wife, who was related to the Hasmoneans, which gave him perceived legitimacy as part of a royal line. Through his dealings with Rome, Herod was granted the title "king of the Jews," ending the Hasmonean era in 37 BC and beginning the Herodian period under Roman oversight. If there was relative peace in the region, and money was sent to Rome, he could do almost as he pleased, and he was pleased to become very wealthy.

Herod was a master builder, which was one way he sought to have his name honored. Among his projects were an immense temple platform, which is there today, and massive improvements to the second temple, which are not. The temple itself echoed the splendor of Solomon, as it literally shone like the sun over Jerusalem. Thousands of priests and Levites rotated through the temple duties, and the nations gathered there. Yet within was spiritual decay, and its Most Holy Place was empty.

Herod is also known as the one who ordered the death of infant sons as a way to protect his throne from Jesus, the coming Messiah.

Now many of the pieces are in place for the New Testament period.

- Synagogues appeared. With people dispersed and temple worship interrupted, the people found synagogues as a way to gather without priests and temple.

- Priests were spiritually unreliable. Some priests were interested in consolidating power and wealth; some were pious seekers of God.

- Priests were more interested in maintaining Jewish identity than in being able to discern sin and being a light to the world.

In all this, there was reason for hope. The Lord still made appearances in his sanctuary (Luke 1:11)—he was never dependent on the presence of the ark. And Israel still looked for a liberator from Rome, the Egypt-like oppressor.

Response

If we notice anything in this history, we see that the Lord is accustomed to entering into very messy situations in which he is uninvited but still faithful to his promises.

PART 2

JESUS OUR TABERNACLE

Descend
Blood
Lamb
CLOSE
Weddings
Touch
Ascend

21

The Holy One Descends

When Jesus came to us in human flesh, the priestly story converged on him. More accurately, the priestly story and every detail of the tabernacle converged on him. Our entire priestly identity would soon be absorbed into his.

Though his birth had more evidence of lowliness than glory, the Gospel of John starts big: "In the beginning was the Word, and the Word was with God, and the Word was God" (John 1:1). From chaos to life, that's what happened in the beginning, and that is what happened in Jesus. Jesus is the creator God, the life, the light, and he has come to re-create a world that has been unraveling. His coming was no mere hovering. It was a full-on intrusion. The light and life entered into our earth, and his words and work will bring the creation to its intended state.

He descended a ladder, or staircase. It had appeared once before, during a time of trouble in Jacob's life. When Jacob saw a ladder, "the angels of God were ascending and descending on it," while the Lord stood above it and spoke (Gen. 28:12–13). The angel's words were full of promises and comfort, and

Jacob renamed the place as a sanctuary of God, which was a forerunner of the first, official tabernacle.

His public ministry began in Galilee where he gathered disciples—Andrew, Peter, and Philip among them. Philip quickly shared the news about Jesus with Nathaniel, who was initially skeptical that the Messiah could be based in Nazareth, but he still approached Jesus. "Jesus saw Nathanael coming toward him and said of him, 'Behold, an Israelite indeed, in whom there is no deceit!'" (John 1:47). "No deceit" refers to Nathanael's character. It also alludes to Jacob, whose name meant deceiver (Gen. 27:35–36). Then Jesus revealed how much had changed since Jacob witnessed the ladder. Jesus said, "Truly, truly, I say to you, you will see heaven opened, and the angels of God ascending and descending on the Son of Man" (John 1:51).

The ladder itself was the same. Angels were freely going between two realms. What was different was that God, once seen at the top of the ladder, was now on earth. The Lord—the Son of Man, the Ancient of Days, Jesus the Christ—had descended in all humility and love. This was always his intent. In the weakness of a baby he gave up power. He came to us, and the distance between heaven and earth has been forever recalibrated.

Response

1. Jesus descended the ladder so that he could set his tent among us (John 1:14).[20] The tent is a reference to the original tabernacle. God had come in the flesh to dwell, once and for all, with his people, which raises questions about the fate of Herod's temple in Jerusalem. With Jesus's coming, the nearness of God was intensified. Does his descent assure you that God is committed to being close to us and drawing us near to him?

2. Jacob was a deceiver; Nathaniel was guileless. They represent the worst and best, but the Lord drew near to both. Do you ever think that you are the exception, and Jesus is reluctant to draw near to you? If so, how do you counter such a lie?

22

Jesus Our Passover Lamb

The fate of the priests is tied to the fate of their temple. In AD 70, the temple in Jerusalem was razed to the ground by Roman armies—the records of the priestly line destroyed with it—and it has not been rebuilt since. John wrote his Gospel around AD 90; the other Gospels were written before AD 70. Therefore both John and his readers knew of the Maccabean-like revolt that aroused Roman ire in AD 66. They knew that in response, Rome's fury landed on the city, and Rome sacked and destroyed the temple. Many had relatives and friends among the thousands of slain citizens.

Afterward they had to wonder what the temple's destruction meant for their life and worship. How would God be present with his people when his house was no longer standing? What would happen to the priesthood? When God's people approached the temple, they had to be clean. Priests did their ceremonial washings on the temple grounds. The rest of the people went to the large pools located near the temple. Without a temple, cleansing seemed irrelevant—why bother getting washed when there was no house of God to approach? But perhaps there was another kind of cleansing available.

John's Gospel quickly introduces us to another John, John the Baptist. He was designated to come ahead of the King and tell everyone to get ready for the King who was coming (Mal. 4:5). They were to prepare by confessing sin, turning from it, and expressing their repentance in baptism. Those steps were the way to greet the King. It was a suitable expression of the deeper cleansing of the soul that was to come, and one didn't have to go to the temple or its pools. It pointed the way to what had been the hope all along:

> I will sprinkle clean water on you, and you shall be clean from all your uncleannesses, and from all your idols I will cleanse you. (Ezek. 36:25)

John the Baptist also baptized Jesus (John 1:32). Jesus's baptism was not for forgiveness of sins. More likely it was Jesus's consecration as God's priest (Ex. 29:4). The event was so important that all four Gospels include it, and it was so important that each text identifies the presence of the Spirit and the Father with the Son. This is the most obvious appearance of the triune God in Scripture. From all eternity, God was close within himself. The Father, Son, and Spirit shared the most intense nearness and friendship. For reasons we will never fully understand, God always planned to bring believing humanity into this divine nearness, and he would do it through the Lamb.

The Baptist introduced the King this way: "Behold, the Lamb of God, who takes away the sin of the world!" (John 1:29). The next day John was with two of his disciples and saw Jesus walk by—an allusion to the God who walked with his people in the garden, at the tabernacle, and here, in person, face-to-face. He said again, "Behold, the Lamb of God" (John

1:36). Since the apostle who wrote these things was interested in evidence and witnesses, he adds that the disciples heard this and followed Jesus.

Jesus is the Creator and King, the light and the life. John has already mentioned these. But Jesus chooses to be known as the Lamb of God, which draws our attention to the Passover. Passover is incorporated into what is usually called the seven-day Feast of Unleavened Bread. It is the first of Israel's feasts both in their history and in their calendar year. The feasts that follow Passover all build on this rescuing work of God and this first corporate call to offer a sacrificed animal. The Day of Atonement is an amplified version of Passover.

The story is well known. It dates back before there was a temple, when the people were in Egyptian bondage, and Pharaoh refused to let the people go. As part of their rescue, the family heads acted as priests and sacrificed a lamb or a young goat. The blood was sprinkled on the family doorposts, and the animal was eaten by the family and invited guests. When the Lord saw the blood, he passed over the house, or, better, he hovered over and guarded the house. He was present with his people and gave them life. Each bloodstained house functioned as a holy place, and the Lord himself stood guard against any sign of death. Meanwhile, he did not protect the houses unmarked by animal sacrifice. Man can only be spared through blood.

In Jesus, the Passover and its feast find their fullest expression. He is the reason for Israel's rescue. Houses were protected in honor of his blood that would later be shed. Jesus is the Passover lamb, and God himself is the one who supplied the lamb. Jesus is God's Lamb.

Abraham pointed to this truth when Isaac was about to become Abraham's lamb, but he received, instead, the ram belonging to and given by God. All the sacrifices Israel ever made point to Jesus, because everything belongs to the Lord, and he provided the sacrificial animals for the people. Jesus, however, is *the* Lamb of God. If there was any doubt, John later tells us that Jesus was taken to his crucifixion during "the day of Preparation" at the same time the Passover lambs were being slaughtered (John 19:14), and, like the Passover lambs, his limbs were not broken (Ex. 12:46; John 19:33).

The world is being renewed, and the temple is where renewal began. Renewal did not begin with revival among the priests or with Jesus installed as high priest. It began with the perfect sacrifice, supplied by God himself, freely offered by the Son. If Jesus were simply an improved priest, he would have restored right worship and right teaching to the temple, and the day-to-day practices would have continued. But because Jesus is the Lamb, there is no more need for temple sacrifices, and when the heavenly court is in session, Satan can no longer raise legitimate accusations against believers.

Response

1. There is only one way, and it is through God's Lamb. This means that we want to speak about this Lamb in ways that are understandable to everyone. How would you describe to a neighbor this way of God's Lamb?

23

Interrupted by a Wedding

John the Baptist and God's Lamb have been introduced. Now the heart of John's Gospel can begin, and it begins like this: "On the third day there was a wedding" (John 2:1).

We are brought into a wedding in progress, on the third day—but on the third day of what? Perhaps John means, on the third day *of* a wedding celebration. Weddings routinely lasted a week, and Jesus was generous to an underprepared wedding host and turned water into wine. The compassion of our High Priest was on display. But John was always aiming for deeper spiritual realities, so we look for more meaning. On the third day, after the resurrection of the Lamb of God, there was a wedding, and the celebration began. John is telling the story in hindsight. His strategy is to start with the death and resurrection of God's Lamb and bring everything into that event.

John's method of counting for this better wedding is anchored in the Passover:

- Day 1: Jesus is crucified on Friday, the day of preparation for Passover.

- Day 2: Jesus "rests" in the tomb on Saturday, the Sabbath.

- Day 3: Jesus is resurrected on Sunday, the first day of the week.

Cleansing water was needed at both Passovers and weddings. At the wedding Jesus attended, there were six 30-gallon jars used for purification, and Jesus chose these as ideally suitable for his purposes—to turn this cleansing water into wine. Wine, at the time of John's writing, was associated with the new covenant in Jesus's blood (1 Cor. 11:25). In other words, cleansing water, which had to be used daily, was replaced by the blood of Jesus, which washes once and for all. Though this message was not available to those at the wedding celebration, it was evident to readers in AD 90, and it is evident to us.

Here is the message: the destruction of our temple still echoes. The pain persists. Some wonder, what is God doing? The answer is that we have the benefits of a fully functioning temple, plus much more. Our rescue and purification are now found in the blood of Jesus, our Passover lamb. We always knew we needed the better lamb given by God. Now, having believed in the Son—fully human and fully God—we no longer are separated from him by walls and curtains. Instead, we are with him and he with us. We are priests together, and we have unlimited access to the Most Holy Place. The closeness has become so intense that it could be described as the joining of a bride with her bridegroom. So, in Christ, we can have joy today.

Yet there is more. Hebrew literature is usually more structured than it first appears. One stylistic flourish is to essentially be able to fold a book in half and have the halves roughly match each other. If a theme in the beginning is important, it will be repeated at the end. If "on the third day" is important, it should have its analog at the end of the book, and it does.

"On the first day of the week . . ."—that's how John finishes his account (John 20:1). This is the same as "the third day," but John's counting method has shifted from the Passover and takes its cue from the seven days of creation, which also have shaped his Gospel.

- Day 6: Adam and Eve are created; Jesus is revealed as "the man" (John 19:5), the second Adam, at his crucifixion.

- Day 7: God rests; Jesus "rests" on the Sabbath.

- Day 1: Re-creation begins. The light dawns. Jesus inaugurates the new creation with his resurrection, and the most intimate of walks await us.

This, writes John, is a new day. The Passover has finally caught up to its true meaning in the sacrifice of God's Lamb. The temple, and its promise of God's presence, has given way to the picture of marriage. We are royal priests, and we are bride priests. Priestly nearness to God cannot quite capture the intimacy that has been God's goal with us, so Scripture is merging another identity. It is not new. The first marriage in the garden mirrored the ways of God with his people. "As the bridegroom rejoices over the bride, so shall your God rejoice over you" (Isa. 62:5).

With this added identity in mind, it is clear that holiness is not our goal. It is a means to an end. God makes us holy, and we grow in holiness; both serve the purpose of our communion with him. This goal of communion is clear from God's presence in the garden (Gen. 3:8); from Jesus's prayer, "I in them and you in me" (John 17:23); and from our marital consummation when Jesus returns (Rev. 21:1–2). Fellowship, bound up with worship, praise, and downright enjoyment, is what we are after.

And it all rests on his nearness and invitation to draw closer. When we are truly human, this is what we want. God's laws, at their best, are instructions about how to be in relationship with him. Like any relationship, the more we follow the rules of the relationship—sexual fidelity, truthfulness, serving in love—the more we know intimacy and pleasure.

Response

1. Jesus is your Passover. What does that mean for you?

2. Jesus is the author of the new creation. How would you describe that, especially when so many things on earth seem to be unchanged?

24

Jesus the Temple

We are in the Gospel of John. The temple is in view. The calendar seems stuck on the Passover.

> The Passover of the Jews was at hand, and Jesus went up to Jerusalem. In the temple he found those who were selling oxen and sheep and pigeons, and the money-changers sitting there. And making a whip of cords, he drove them all out of the temple. (John 2:13–15)

The temple platform was a vast expanse. The temple itself and its courts were walled and reserved for Israelites. Gentiles were permitted in a large courtyard that was beyond these walls. It was in this area, open to all worshipers, that Jesus confronted those who sold sacrificial animals and exchanged foreign currency.

The problem seems to have been that the commerce interfered with Gentile worship. The temple was intended to be a light to the nations, and people were being kept away. The place of worship had become a marketplace. As Jesus was angry when children were kept from him, so he was angry when the nations were kept from seeking the Lord.

But it is the next part of this story that catches our attention. When the Jews asked about his authority for taking such action, Jesus's response revealed that his death and resurrection were always his plan:

> "Destroy this temple, and in three days I will raise it up." The Jews then said, "It has taken forty-six years to build this temple, and will you raise it up in three days?" But he was speaking about the temple of his body. (John 2:19–21)

Jesus was not speaking in parables here. The magnificent Jerusalem temple, rebuilt by Herod, would be destroyed, but *the* temple—the very body of Jesus—would not be destroyed but would be raised from the dead to be the living temple, and we would join him.

> The stone that the builders rejected has become the cornerstone; this was the Lord's doing, and it is marvelous in our eyes. (Matt. 21:42)

Jesus *is* the temple, John writes. God's signposts have always pointed to Jesus. The temple is a copy; Jesus is the original. Worship is now centered on him. His body and his blood became our way to pass through the veil that quarantined the Most Holy Place. If you want to see something more magnificent than the glimmering temple that once stood over all Jerusalem, look at Jesus.

Response

If anything is becoming clear, it is that the Son has been put forward in a way that shows how human history and our personal identity are wrapped up in him.

[The Father] put all things under his [Jesus's] feet and gave him as head over all things to the church, which is his body, the fullness of him who fills all in all. (Eph. 1:22–23)

Jesus is the Passover. Now Jesus is the temple. What difference does that make for you?

25

Jesus the High Priest

The temple and all its furnishings and sacrifices were copies or images of Jesus. Priests too are in the image of Christ. When the apostle John received "the revelation of Jesus Christ" (Rev. 1:1), Jesus is in his holy house, by the golden lampstand and dressed in priestly garments (Rev. 1:12–13). But Jesus is rarely identified as the high priest in the New Testament because he is actually from a different line of priests.

Lineage was all-important for the priests, especially the high priests. Jesus, however, was from Judah, not Levi and Aaron. He had kings in his line but not priests. So Hebrews 7 makes the case that Jesus, indeed, has a lineage. He came from the more exalted order of Melchizedek:

> The LORD has sworn
>   and will not change his mind,
> "You are a priest forever
>   after the order of Melchizedek. (Ps. 110:4)

Our high priest is from the earth. Jesus, like Melchizedek, shares our humanity; he is of the earth. He experienced

weakness and need. He knows the strength of the temptations that assault our souls. So expect gentleness from him,
and mercy. The priests began their day with sacrifices for their
own sins. Jesus the high priest was sinless so did not offer up
sacrifices for his own cleansing, but he did offer up desperate
prayers to the Father as death surrounded him (Heb. 5:7). So
we can draw near to him.

Our high priest is from heaven. We are of mixed lineage,
both of earth and of heaven. The Aaronic priesthood had much
of earth but little of heaven, so another line of priests was in
order. Melchizedek was Jesus. He was greater than Aaron. The
writer of Hebrews argues that Aaron, through his ancestor
Abraham, actually paid tithes to this greater priest who was
"without father or mother or genealogy, having neither beginning of days nor end of life" (Heb. 7:3).

Our high priest is our king from heaven. He alone has authority. For example, the priests of Jesus's day had refined a
series of laws about what to eat and who to eat with. These
became a significant feature of Hebrew identity and were used
as evidence for the superiority of Jews over Gentiles. One reason Jesus was considered unfit to be the Messiah was that he
ignored these laws and ate with "tax collectors and sinners"
(Matt. 9:10–11). In this he revealed himself as the new high
priest who redrew the boundaries of clean and unclean. The
clean were those who knew they were unclean, came to Jesus
and believed in him, and followed him in obedience to the
Father (Matt. 15:10–20; Mark 7:18–23).

Not only does Jesus show from his authority that he is from
God; Jesus our high priest is also the God who is eternal. He
came from heaven as part of the royal priestly line of Melchizedek, and he has entered back into the heavens. Whereas sickness, age, and death terminated the work of all other priests,
Jesus is the living priest who offered his own body as the once-

for-all sacrifice. He sprinkled or smeared his own blood on the altar and the mercy seat in a way that our sins are actually covered by that smeared blood. Then he sat down, retiring the entire temple system (Heb. 1:3; 10:12). He still functions as our active high priest, but he is in the heavens, at the right hand of the Father, assuring us that heaven, his very home, is our home.

God's presence in Eden's garden, no matter how nice, were merely *visits* from which Jesus returned to heaven. Man was landlocked, always at the bottom of the ladder. A mere earthly high priest could not change that. It would take one who was *both* from heaven and from earth. Only then could we be represented by the perfect human and brought into heaven by the true God.

Response

You are familiar with some parts of your family tree, such as your parents and grandparents. Maybe you can trace your line back for generations, but this biological part of your identity has been surpassed by a better one. The "from heaven" is now primary. You have been born of Melchizedek, born of Jesus, born of God. Your most enduring identity is that you are descended from Jesus. This was the crux of the conversation between Jesus and Nicodemus.

> Truly, truly, I say to you, unless one is born of water and the Spirit, he cannot enter the kingdom of God. That which is born of the flesh is flesh, and that which is born of the Spirit is spirit. (John 3:5–6)

Can you tell your own story this way?

26

Believe

With the temple and its sacrifices fulfilled in Jesus, the way to be cleansed and close to God is to follow him.

In short, it's to believe.

The apostle John compiled the evidence, one sign after another. Signs are "moments when heaven and earth is opened, when the transforming power of God's love bursts in to the present world."[21] Signs are when heaven and earth meet, when God's glory appears, and, as witnesses to that glory, we believe.

The first sign was when Jesus changed water to wine. In this he revealed his glory—that he was from God and was God—and "his disciples believed in him" (John 2:11).

Other signs followed. Jesus healed a nobleman's son without even seeing him, and the nobleman believed (4:46–54). He healed a lame man on the Sabbath, and the divide became more evident between those who believed and those who did not (5:1–17). He fed five thousand people from a boy's lunch, and many believed, though some were more interested in the bread (6:1–15). He healed a man born blind, and even though a formal inquiry verified the healing, the leaders closed their eyes and ears to the sign. Meanwhile, the once-blind man said, " 'Lord, I believe' and worshiped him" (9:38).

The last sign before his crucifixion, the raising of Lazarus from the dead, was crammed with the call to believe:

- The reason for Lazarus's death was so Jesus could reveal his glory, that is, his very identity (11:4).

- Jesus became very specific with Martha, Lazarus's sister. "Jesus said to her, 'I am the resurrection and the life. Whoever believes in me, though he die, yet shall he live, and everyone who lives and believes in me shall never die'" (11:25–26).

- Jesus asked Martha a specific question: "'Do you believe this?' She said to him, 'Yes, Lord; I believe that you are the Christ, the Son of God, who is coming into the world'" (11:26–27).

- Many did, indeed, believe, and this groundswell of support for Jesus is what led to specific plans for his death.

If there is any doubt that believing is the way to God's presence, John summarized his entire Gospel as a call to us to believe:

Now Jesus did many other signs in the presence of the disciples, which are not written in this book; but these are written so that you may believe that Jesus is the Christ, the Son of God, and that by believing you may have life in his name. (John 20:30–31)

This focus on believing was not new. We find it in the Old Testament too: "Believe in the LORD your God, and you will be established" (2 Chron. 20:20). Yet the history of Israel is that they did not believe, in spite of the evidence of God's love and power. Today, however, is a new day with new power that comes from the Spirit. So John wants us to act. Now is the time.

These are just a few of the signs that Jesus is the one who descended from heaven. They all point to the glory of the Lamb slain for us. Look at the signs. Listen to his words. Then believe. Acknowledge who Jesus claims to be. Turn away from seeking the glory of reputation and seek the glory of his presence and boast in his reputation.

John puts the question before us: "Do you believe that he is the one sent by the Father?" A simple response of believing becomes a sign both to ourselves and to the world that we belong to the family of God through Jesus. If you believe him, you belong to him. This means that your earthly line has been usurped by the heavenly. You are "born again" or "born from above" (John 3:3). Marriage again captures it. "I believe" is the same as "I do." It is a public declaration of our allegiances. It announces our oneness with a spouse. It engrafts us into the line of our bridegroom. There is much that happens with a simple, "I believe."

Believing, however, has always been less steady than we would like. In John's day, some believed Jesus, then turned away, never to return. They were hoping for something more than a crucified rescuer. They wanted the earthly, the guarantee of bread or political safety, more than the heavenly, life with Christ in a world of uncertainty and rejection. When life became either better or worse, they didn't believe. Yet others did believe. They felt a bit shaky in their belief, and they asked for Jesus's help, and even the disciples turned from Jesus when fear overtook them. But those who believe in Jesus return to Jesus, and they grow from their lapses by listening to his word and remembering the signs.

So true worship is founded on believing what God has said and done. That has always been the foundation of life with

God. As Jesus said to the Samaritan woman, you don't have to be close to Jerusalem. Rather, you come to Christ, the living water, the living tabernacle. You come to him, the truth, the embodiment of the invisible spirit God who cannot be contained by a temple.

Response

1. What are you saying when you say with Martha, "Yes, Lord; I believe that you are the Christ, the Son of God, who is coming into the world"?

2. Consider speaking Martha's words, "I believe that you are the Christ, the Son of God, who is coming into the world," to the Lord each day for the next week.

27

Descending Further

With the temple mobile in the person of Jesus, we learn more about God and his ways. Even when toddlers begin to walk, we learn more about their tendencies and what is especially important to them—stairs, a particular person, an electrical outlet. When we watch Jesus, the ways of God become especially vivid.

First, he descended. He left heaven and encamped on earth:

> Christ Jesus, who, though he was in the form of God, did not count equality with God a thing to be grasped, but emptied himself, by taking the form of a servant, being born in the likeness of men. (Phil. 2:6–7)

His descent confirms his promise to come near to his people. He did not wait for us to come up to him. He descended to us in gentleness and humility. We have no reason to be afraid but every reason to come.

Then the ladder went wherever we might be found. He passed by the smug and arrogant, and he stopped and spoke to the ones no one else saw. He looked ordinary—rejected, and with nothing that suggests majesty and kingly authority. Those who went looking for him had to look for the least likely person:

> He had no form or majesty that we should look at him,
>   and no beauty that we should desire him.
> He was despised and rejected by men;
>   a man of sorrows and acquainted with grief;
> and as one from whom men hide their faces he was
>   despised,
>   and we esteemed him not. (Isa. 53:2–3)

His glory was apparent to those whose daily life was full of shame. It was veiled from those who felt no need for rescue. This is how they recognized him: "The blind receive their sight, the lame walk, lepers are cleansed, and the deaf hear, the dead are raised up, the poor have good news preached to them" (Luke 7:22)—to which we would add, those who have been shamefully violated by others and those whose sins seemed beyond the pale. With all these, Jesus not only came near, but he touched them. He touched lepers, the blind, the sick, and even the dead. He touched children who, though not necessarily unclean, were considered to be of little worth. Those who were touched knew that this was not merely a sign of affection but that Jesus identified with them, and they knew that his touch could give life, which meant that it announced forgiveness. Once word got around, people who understood his love and power were trying to touch him.

Two stories capture this intimate descent. In the first, a woman whose sins were well known in the community—an untouchable—came to a place where Jesus had been invited for a meal (Luke 7:36–50). Having already understood his forgiving touch, she naturally went closer. She wept in gratitude even to the point where her tears wet his feet; she wiped her tears with her hair, kissed his feet, and then anointed his feet with her ointment. It was a scandalous act to those present—she in all her touchy-feely uncleanness. But she is praised and identified as one who believed and is to be emulated.

The other story is a woman who was far from God because of her bleeding rather than her sin. In other words, our distance from God can be a result of our sin or any association with death such as sickness and even victimization, in that abusers are connected to Satan, who is the power behind death. This woman was unclean because of what had happened to her (Luke 8:43–48). She knew of Jesus's reputation—"she had heard the reports" (Mark 5:27)—though she herself had never been close to him. She approached him anonymously, from behind, confident that his mission was to snatch his people from death and bring life, and she was right. A simple touch stopped her uncleanness.

Jesus used the moment to reveal the deeper meaning of what happened. She had laid hands on God's Lamb and transferred her uncleanness to him, and the Lamb had given his power and life to her while he went off into the wilderness bearing the weight of sin, shame, sickness, and everything connected to death.

Why her? Why was she the one who received life while so many were pressing on Jesus? She believed. She believed that he was the anointed one sent by the Father. She needed him, and only he could give life.

In his descent Jesus invites us to touch him, and we can be sure that he will descend wherever we are.

His descent continued. At the Passover meal with his disciples, he became the servant who washed their feet (John 13:1–20). In turns out that a requirement for being close to him is that you let him serve you. Here again, the apostle John crams meaning into an event. Jesus was both host and servant. As host, he supplied for us the meal of his very body and blood. As servant, he washed the feet of weary travelers. He also washed the day's debris of sin from those who believed.

And the ladder went into death itself. God's Lamb always took aim at death, which means he took aim at sin, Satan, and death. So much of his descent was in order to be with us, and we with him, but this final descent he took by himself, for us, so that we would never know life alone.

The story of God is a story of descent. We might have missed that during the tabernacle and temple periods, but looking back, we see that the tabernacle was, indeed, God descending. He pursued his people for forty years in a harsh wilderness, never leaving their side. The movement from heaven to earth was always natural to him.

Response

1. We can sometimes believe that our sins are too bad and our shame is beyond cleansing or covering. As a way to prepare for such times, consider those two heroic women. They were witnesses to Jesus's love, power, and descent. How do they encourage your faith in Jesus?

2. How does Jesus's descent lead you to love him and worship?

28

The Lamb Slain

Priests worked where heaven came to earth. From that vantage point they were in a position to understand the ways of God as they carried out their temple duties. Everything was up close. If they had eyes to see and ears to hear, this is what they saw and what they knew:

- God worked through priestly representatives who experienced his cleansing and closeness on behalf of all the people. One high priest represented the people on the Day of Atonement. When he entered the two rooms of God's temple, the people entered with him. Priestly representatives assured the people that cleansing was possible for all.

- God worked through representatives or substitutes who experienced God's wrath against rebellion and contempt. God accepted animals as a substitute. Food could be offered as secondary offerings of thanks and fellowship, but only blood could cover sins. "Without the shedding of blood there is no forgiveness of sins" (Heb. 9:22).

- Blood was shorthand for life, and this life poured out but not the blood of God's people. Though our many sins demand that our life be poured out, the blood of an animal temporarily stood in man's place.

- The blood of animals was not the final word. An animal could not ultimately stand in for a human because animals are not like humans. And what would priests do when the temple no longer existed and they had no legitimate way to sacrifice? Though thankful for animal substitutes, they always knew that the sacrifices pointed to something else.

- The Day of Atonement was always in view. This was the day that the high priest entered the Most Holy Place and fulfilled the goal of humanity, which was to be with God. Blood was sprinkled throughout the tabernacle as a way to say that the entire world needed cleansing—God was doing more than giving a local or tribal blessing. Then the sin offering added a live goat to be sent away, an exiled substitute so that God's people could stay close.

- The prophet Isaiah saw more (Isa. 39–53). The coming Messiah would be the servant representative of the people, and he would bring good news, but he'd be despised by the people. He would take our sins and sorrows on himself so that we could know peace; he would bear God's wrath for us, and his shed blood would extend to all the nations. The people understood the words, "His soul makes an offering for guilt" (53:10), but they had no precedent for understanding how a human being would take the place of the lambs and bulls. The convergence of high exaltation, thoroughgoing oppression, and suffering in extremis are almost impossible for human minds to hold together.

All creation had been waiting for a new Adam—a new priest—to introduce a new creation. Noah was a possibility but failed. Abraham was also a candidate, but he died, and his progeny were clearly not a new humanity. Yet Abraham was more promising than he seemed. He exemplified the way of believing. Perfection was not available to a mere human, but believing in the perfect faithfulness of God was possible. Harder to understand was God's descending as the one both spotless and disgraced.

Believe that he is the one from heaven, sent from the Father—that is what he asks of us. Confess your need for help and rescue. Awake from your slumber, wrote the apostle Paul.

Jesus was the true human being, our suitable representative, and the true God who alone could give us life and bring us with him into heaven. For this to happen, he joined himself to us, took everything of ours that was associated with death, gave everything of his that was associated with life, and brought our death to its rightful end.

As God tends to do, the announcement of his ways comes from unlikely people.

> So Jesus came out, wearing the crown of thorns and the purple robe. Pilate said to them, "Behold the man!" (John 19:5)

Pilate proclaimed that Jesus was the man initiating a new sixth day in which a new humanity would be formed around him and brought into God's rest and peace. All we can do is agree—believe—that Jesus is, indeed, the man and God, and his death becomes our peace.

Response

When we consider our identity as priests, we are signing on to more deeply understand "Jesus died for my sins."

Why could Jesus alone die in our place?

Why did he die?

What difference does his death make?

What might the apostle Paul mean when he writes that we are "in Christ"? (Rom. 8:1; 1 Cor. 1:30; 2 Cor. 5:17)

29

Jesus Ascends, the Spirit Descends

No one anticipated that the Christ would descend as far down as the outcasts and the unclean, and then into death itself. And no one anticipated that death would not hold him. It had never happened before. Even when Lazarus was raised from death to life, death still had the final say. But Jesus had said, "No one has ascended into heaven except he who descended from heaven, the Son of Man" (John 3:13). Whoever believes in him ascends with him. He was even more explicit later: "The Son of Man is going to be delivered into the hands of men, and they will kill him. And when he is killed, after three days he will rise" (Mark 9:31).

There have been many deaths more gruesome than Jesus's death. There have been more painful deaths, and tortures that lasted longer. But it is the resurrection that makes Jesus's death the most meaningful and dense with spiritual realities. The Father raised Jesus in order to authenticate his approval for the work of the Son. The resurrection declared to the world that

Jesus—and Jesus alone—is the eternal Son of God, and Jesus alone has all rights to the heavenly realms and can bring people to God (Rom. 1:4).

He descended alone, then the Spirit rested on him and empowered him throughout his life on earth. When he ascended, he was by no means alone. God always intended to have his people near, and in Christ they would be brought to him:

> Believe in God; believe also in me. In my Father's house are many rooms. If it were not so, would I have told you that I go to prepare a place for you? And if I go and prepare a place for you, I will come again and will take you to myself, that where I am you may be also. (John 14:1–3)

His ascension was first announced to Mary, when he appeared to her at the tomb. "Jesus said to her, 'Do not cling to me, for I have not yet ascended to the Father; but go to my brothers and say to them, "I am ascending to my Father and your Father, to my God and your God"'" (John 20:17). Perhaps Jesus was saying that his stay with her would be temporary because he would ultimately ascend and not return. Then, for forty days, he appeared to move freely between heaven and earth, teaching, eating, and "speaking about the kingdom of God" (Acts 1:3).

After forty days he ascended to prepare a home for his people, not to return until his final coming. He ascended to the throne that was over all the demonic usurpers. Satan and his accomplices always had death as evidence of their power. Physical death and our fears of death were a summary of their province, which included everything linked to death such as sin, victimization, sickness, hatred, and all things opposed to God. When Jesus conquered death, he conquered all these. This was the beginning of creation being brought back to its proper head so that nothing could separate us from God, and, instead of heaven and earth having a mere point of contact, heaven would fill the entire earth in Jesus:

> [The father] raised him from the dead and seated him at his right hand in the heavenly places, far above all rule and authority and power and dominion, and above every name that is named, not only in this age but also in the one to come. And he put all things under his feet and gave him as head over all things to the church, which is his body, the fullness of him who fills all in all. (Eph. 1:20–22)

The final act of his ascension and coronation was the Spirit, received from the Father, poured out on us (Acts 2:2–3). Kings typically receive gifts when they ascend to the throne; Jesus gave himself as the gift, and the Spirit binds us to Jesus. This happened during the Feast of Weeks, or Pentecost, fifty days after the crucifixion. The feast was a time of thanksgiving for what God had done and doubled both as a harvest festival and a time to remember the giving of the law on Sinai. Jesus had gathered the primary festivals into himself: Passover and the associated feast of unleavened bread, the Day of Atonement and the associated Feast of Booths, and Pentecost.

This Pentecost revealed that the heavenly ladder remained a busy one. After Jesus ascended, the Spirit descended. In his descent he gives power to his people, groans on our behalf before the throne, and brings us into Jesus so that we abide in him. The Spirit has raised us with Jesus (Rom. 8:11). As a result, it is now official. We are no longer citizens of earth, nor do we have dual citizenship. Instead, we are strangers and aliens on earth, and we are full citizens of heaven as we wait with Christ for the day when he will bring heaven to earth (Phil. 3:20). Meanwhile, the Spirit brings us up the ladder and unites us to the risen Jesus.

Response

1. The old priestly stories seem to have some advantages: you can *see* them. You can see the garments and the minimalist furnishings of the tabernacle. You can smell the incense. But at this point we have moved into a realm in which seeing is more difficult. The story is now much better, but it is spiritual. In other words, it feels otherworldly and somehow more like clouds than tangible realities. *Spiritual*, however, usually means "from the Spirit," and it is about rock-solid permanence. What we see will fade, but what we don't see is certain and eternal. As with all dramatic changes, this one takes reminders and meditation and the help of others in order to see clearly. There is, indeed, a ladder, an inheritance, and life resides there. The evidence of that heavenly life appears when you ask forgiveness from God or others, or when you love though it might be costly. Find it when you pray, "My Father." How are you seeing heavenly realities in your everyday life?

2. Read Ephesians 1:1–14, Paul's psalm about the resurrection and its impact.

PART 3

ALMOST TRULY HUMAN

Ascend
Eternal
Life
Spirit
IN CHRIST
CHRIST IN US
Saints
Love
Permanence
Reflect

30

Priests in Plain Clothes

Today's priests wear ordinary clothes, work in ordinary jobs, and are hard to single out. They are subject to the same losses and hardships as the rest of the world. They are more likely to feel substandard than holy. This is what happens when we are being organized around the High Priest who was rejected and poor. We have entered into life itself, yet death—as loss, broken relationships, and broken bodies—still surrounds us.

Priests are needy. Poor and needy—that is how it typically feels to be a priest.

> As for me, I am poor and needy,
>   but the LORD takes thought for me.
> You are my help and my deliverer;
>   do not delay, O my God (Ps. 40:17)

This is the cry of the Old Testament saints, and it was the cry of Jesus. Saints in the New Testament were needy too. You can identify them as those who put their faith in Jesus instead of in other people or in themselves. Many were sick (Luke 8:48; 18:42), some were known by their sins (Luke 7:5; 19:9), others were societal outcasts (Luke 18:14), and one was a Roman centurion counted among the pagan dogs (Matt. 8:8). To this group we could add the first disciples, who were undereducated men of no particular importance and uneven character. These are the heroes we aspire to be like. They knew that they could not manage life on their own. Their sins and troubles were too great. They saw the pretense in flaunting personal righteousness or other works that could gather bits of prestige. They saw in Jesus the one who both invited them to draw near and had the power to help. Their faith was simply, "I need you." This, of course, is not natural to us and is evidence of the Spirit's power at work, and it is the way of drawing near to God.

Priests believe. What consecrates us as priests is that we believe in Jesus. This belief is not a less-than-rational leap into the unknown, as in, "You just have to believe." Instead, we have seen the signs that he is from heaven and is God in the flesh. Belief has its reasons.

Notice how humans have always invented gods who look like themselves though a little stronger. No one anticipated the God who was weak more than strong, humble more than heroic. Jesus might not be what we expected, but he is what we hoped for. He is unmoved by flashy displays of personal worth. His humility and gentleness attract children, misfits, the unwashed, and those with immoral pasts. He gives up his power rather than uses it for his advantage. When he uses it, he uses it to serve. Then we see that abundant life follows in his path—sins are forgiven, sicknesses are healed. Death is pushed back. This life appears when there is some evidence that people see their need and recognize that he uniquely can help. So we believe in him and everything he says.

Notice how this story of the priestly identity is unfolding. It began with intimate walks with God. Then it was temporarily licensed to the Hebrew priesthood. The details of that era shed more light on the meaning of the gospel, but the Old Testament priestly activity was so distant from life today. In other words, you might have trouble identifying with the Old Testament priests. Now that the priestly identity has been democratized and redistributed to us all, we find that it can seem quite ordinary until we get more of the knack of living by faith.

Response

1. Which plainclothes priests do you know whose identity is especially obvious?

2. When do you see that your priestly life is anything but ordinary?

31

Priests Descend and Ascend

Belief or faith in Jesus means that we belong to him and he to us. Where he goes, we go. The dilemma is that Jesus is in heaven and we are on earth, which seems far rather than close. This, of course, brings us to the work of the Spirit. Because of Jesus we have the Spirit, and because of the Spirit we have Jesus. To have one is to have the other. The Spirit "declines to disclose himself . . . apart from Christ."[22] The Spirit is the one who keeps us tethered to the living Jesus. God's love is poured out to us "through the Holy Spirit" (Rom. 5:5). To walk in Christ is to walk according to the Spirit (Rom. 8:4). The Spirit brings us into God in such a way that we participate in his plans. Everything we have is in Christ and through the Spirit who dwells in us.

Though this might seem like a stopgap measure until we see Jesus face-to-face, we now have the ways of heaven on earth. Jesus himself experienced unity with the Father by the Spirit. His miracles were by the Spirit. His resurrection was by the Spirit. For us, life in the Spirit will continue even into heaven itself, which helps us to understand how we can have the presence of the physical Christ even when there is space between us. The Spirit is the one who brings us into the Father and the Son.

Jesus descended to give himself to us and bring us to God. For this descent to be meaningful and personal to us, the Spirit, as a witness to this descent, opens our eyes to know Jesus and joins us to him. The Spirit makes Jesus's descent and ascent our own. By the Spirit, Jesus touches us, and we touch him. By the Spirit, Jesus binds himself to us. In this union, we have gone down even into his death:

> I have been crucified with Christ. It is no longer I who live, but Christ who lives in me. And the life I now live in the flesh I live by faith in the Son of God, who loved me and gave himself for me. (Gal. 2:20)

In this death you have been freed from all claims that were rightly against you. The demands of justice in the heavenly court have been fully met, and sin, death, and Satan have lost their power. You have been a real participant in the death of Jesus by the Spirit, though Jesus's separation from the Father was uniquely his own. He did that *for* you rather than with you. Death is now, as Paul wrote, without its sting (1 Cor. 15:55). It is horrible and unnatural in the way it temporarily separates you from those you love, but it is without the sting of judgment or separation from the God of life.

Then up the ladder you go because of the fusing power of the Spirit: "If we have been united with him in a death like his, we shall certainly be united with him in a resurrection like his" (Rom. 6:5). With your old life behind you, you can "walk in newness of life" (Rom. 6:4), which is a life of fellowship with Jesus by the Spirit. Jesus has ascended and is preparing your heavenly dwelling (John 14:2). Your life with him is secure. Meanwhile, the Spirit has made you *his* dwelling (2 Cor. 1:22), which is intimacy and closeness at their most intense.

Our descent and ascent with Jesus is a one-time event. But that event is so pivotal and resounding that it is a pattern that goes through our lives. Think of the exodus from Egypt and the wilderness journey. These were one-time events, but the themes of each recur in Scripture and in life.

We all know the taste of descent. "Man is born to trouble as the sparks fly upward" (Job 5:7). We descend with Christ by the Spirit, which means that we become familiar with failure and rejection. There is trouble in daily life. We also love and serve people who do not love and serve us back. This descent is hard, but when we know that it follows Jesus's lead and is done with him, and that his Spirit is with us to give more life and power, then we can find comfort and even fuller life in it.

Weakness was one way the apostle Paul described his life. He had prayed for the alleviation of his own weakness and suffering, and, given Jesus's many healings, he anticipated relief. When his suffering persisted, he reinterpreted his life with Christ as a descent and ascent:

> He was crucified in weakness, but lives by the power of God. For we also are weak in him, but in dealing with you we will live with him by the power of God. (2 Cor. 13:4)

Strength in weakness. Dependence on God in weakness. This, he understood, was life close to Jesus Christ. That movement from weakness to strength and death to life then became the way he told his own story:

> For his sake I have suffered the loss of all things and count them as rubbish . . . —that I may know him and the power of his resurrection, and may share his sufferings, becoming like him in his death, that by any means possible I may attain the resurrection from the dead. (Phil. 3:8, 10–11)

The life of God's priests on earth is full of reminders that we are expatriates who live at the bottom of the ladder but are citizens of heaven. So life is full of daily hardships and death's leftovers, yet it is also marked by life and love—love from God, love for God, and love toward God's people. And where there is love, expect joy. "These things I have spoken to you, that my joy may be in you, and that your joy may be full" (John 15:11).

Response

1. It is hard to understand how we live at the bottom of the ladder, but our life is actually tucked away with Jesus in his house. Such is the imagination-defying power of the Spirit at work. The Spirit truly brings us into God's house now. We travel the ladder. Heaven is apparent in God's people every day. Every intention, word, and deed that is shaped by our faith in Jesus and the Spirit's work in us is evidence of our heavenly residence. How would you retell your own story as Paul did?

2. The writer of Hebrews wrote, "Let us draw near" (Heb. 10:22). He immediately followed that with, "Let us hold fast the confession of our hope" (v. 23). What words would you use to identify that hope?

32

Saints

The New Testament is reluctant to give us the actual name *priest*. We are, indeed, "a holy priesthood" (1 Pet. 2:5), "a royal priesthood" (1 Pet. 2:9), and "priests to our God" (Rev. 1:6; 5:10; 20:6). Though the apostle Paul was from the tribe of Benjamin and not the priestly tribe of Levi, he describes himself as "a minister of Christ Jesus to the Gentiles in the priestly service of the gospel of God, so that the offering of the Gentiles may be acceptable, sanctified by the Holy Spirit" (Rom. 15:16). Those are most of the direct New Testament references to our priestly identity. We would expect it to appear more often. Not only does the New Testament seem to under-emphasize it, which is surprising given the amount of priestly *imagery* and *echoes* that run throughout, but the church also avoided it for its first two centuries.

No doubt there were reasons. By the time of the cruci-fixion, God's people could not proudly wear the name of *priest* because priests were not, on the whole, an admirable group. The title *priest* had become connected to power and pride. The early church, however, *did* immediately adopt a priestly name as its preferred way of identifying fellow Christians—*saint*.

Saint means "holy one," from the Latin *sanctus*. Our priestly identity resides in the word *holy*. The engraving on the high priest's turban was "Holy to the LORD" (Ex. 28:36). Priests were always set apart or holy to the Lord. The people too were brought into this holiness (Deut. 7:6), and they were brought into God even more when the priestly mantle fell on all who trusted Jesus and followed him through the temple veil, into the Most Holy Place, which was essentially the way to heaven itself.

You are a holy one, a saint. It appears over sixty times in the New Testament. It is always used for *all* the members of God's house.

This identity has always joined two meanings. First, it is the mission of the Holy God to bring people close to himself and to enter into his holiness. You belong to God, and everything that belongs to him carries the imprint of his holiness. Second, it is the mission of God that we grow into that holiness and become holy. As with marriage, you enter into marriage, then you live it out with increasingly more faithfulness, wisdom, and love. Scripture sometimes emphasizes that God is the one who makes us holy. Other times it assumes that because he has set us apart, we become increasingly more like him:

> For you are a people holy to the LORD your God. The LORD your God has chosen you to be a people for his treasured possession, out of all the peoples who are on the face of the earth. (Deut. 7:6)

> O LORD, who shall sojourn in your tent?
> Who shall dwell on your holy hill?
> He who walks blamelessly and does what is right
> and speaks truth in his heart. (Ps. 15:1–2)

You are a holy one. Other identities orbit our holy identity and express how God has brought us close to himself and made us holy:

Members of God's household (Eph. 2:19)
Chosen (1 Pet. 2:4)
Precious (1 Pet. 2:4)
His own possession (1 Pet. 2:9)
Rich (Dan. 7:18)
Servant of God (Titus 1:1; Rev. 1:6)
Friend of God (John 15:15)

And there are more identities to come.

Response

Try wearing the identity *saint*. It removes some of the awkward connotations of *priest* and emphasizes the heart of priestly identity, which is how you have been drawn very near to the Holy One.

33

Shining Faces

Here is another image that comes out of your identity as a saint.

When Jesus suddenly appeared in dazzling white (Luke 9:2–8), his identity as the true God was clear. But mere humanity was dazzling at least once before.

Moses had been invited up the ladder in face-to-face meetings with God. When he came down from those meetings at Sinai, he "did not know that the skin of his face shone because he had been talking with God" (Ex. 34:29). This is humanity as God intended.

At first, this reflected glory kept people at a distance. But Aaron and the other leaders met with the radiant Moses and pronounced him safe, so the people began to go near him. Then Moses told them the words that God had given him. He did this while still shiny. Only when he had finished speaking did he put a veil over his face (Ex. 34:33). Moses wore the veil because the reflected glory of God on his face was fading, which might have discouraged God's people. But there was no need to worry. When Moses spoke to the Lord again, his face shone with refreshed glory.

Moses went into the further reaches of God's house on earth and took on something of God's appearance, which was certainly priest-like. The priests wore clothes that reflected something of God's glory, and here Moses was briefly robed in light. This is image-bearing imitation at its finest. He was that angled mirror who reflected God and illustrated how we are changed by his nearness.

- Moses reflected light because God is light—darkness is associated with fear and hidden dangers.

- Lamps in the Holy Place, which symbolized God's presence, were always lit facing the bread, which symbolized the people.

- The Lord has made his light to shine upon us (Ps. 118:27).

- Jesus himself is the light that shines in darkness (Matt. 4:16).

- Jesus will be our sun when we are with him face-to-face (Rev. 22:5).

- We pray, "Lift up the light of your face upon us, O Lord" (Ps. 4:6), and he does.

The apostle Paul could not resist the picture of the radiant Moses (2 Cor. 3:12–18). His point is that the reflected glory of Christ in his people is better than Moses. Jesus brought us into a new era in which the Spirit opens our eyes to the glory of Jesus. The Spirit also assures us that the glory reflected in us will never fade:

> Since we have such a hope, we are very bold, not like Moses, who would put a veil over his face so that the Israelites might not gaze at the outcome of what was being brought to an end. . . . But when one turns to the Lord, the

veil is removed. . . . And we all, with unveiled face, behold-
ing the glory of the Lord, are being transformed into the
same image from one degree of glory to another. For this
comes from the Lord who is the Spirit. (2 Cor. 3:12–18)

The Spirit brings you into the presence of God, and you
shine as you reflect the light of Jesus. As with holiness, you
have it, and you can grow in it. When you believe, you receive
the Spirit, who shines the light of Christ in you. You can also
grow "from one degree of glory to another" as you continue
to draw near to him.

I saw someone shine today. He is in his fifties, divorced
years ago, and lives in a small efficiency apartment. He has
poor health that limits what he can do. When he gets up in
the morning, he struggles to find any purpose. So he opens
his Bible. Then he reads until he has seen Jesus in Scripture.
Sometimes it takes fifteen minutes, sometimes an hour or more.

Then he shines bright. He is quick to talk about Jesus with
those he meets. If you ask what he is learning, you will be part
of a lively conversation that is filled with hope. Today he spoke
about Jesus as the bread of life from John 6, and we considered
Jesus's call to come to him and believe.

I saw another shiny person. Life has been hard for her, and
she has grumbled along the way. This time, her car had broken
down in a place that blocked traffic, and the breakdown was
going to be costly. "I believe this is God testing me. So instead
of complaining, I am going to be thankful." She had placed her
story right into the pages of Scripture.

A critical event in Israel's history was when the people
grumbled against Moses and Aaron for leading them out of
Egypt (Num. 14:1–4). Even though the Lord had liberated
them with mighty acts, they were essentially asking, "What
have you done for me today?" They complained against
Moses and Aaron, but they were actually standing over God in

judgment. The Lord said to Moses, "How long will this people despise me? And how long will they not believe in me, in spite of all the signs that I have done among them?" (Num. 14:11).

This particular woman, on the day of her car breaking down, would have none of that. Instead, with her eyes set on Jesus, she was patient and thankful.

> Do all things without grumbling or disputing, that you may be blameless and innocent, children of God without blemish in the midst of a crooked and twisted generation, among whom you shine as lights in the world. (Phil. 2:14–15)

It turns out that there are shiny priests around us most every day who follow the course of faith and love in ways that make them appear spectacular and beautiful as they reflect the character of the Lord.

Response

1. You shine when you are brought into Jesus by faith, and you shine even more as you turn toward him. How can this truth be an incentive to move out into the world in the name of Jesus?

2. Who have you seen shine recently?

34

Living Stones,
Flowing Fountains

You are a saint robed in righteousness who reflects Christ with a shining face. Scripture uses an array of images to help us see our saintly identity. Another is that you are a *living* stone. The tradition is ancient. When God came close, people used stones to memorialize the event (e.g., Gen. 28:22). Those fragile heaps were the forerunners of the stones of the temple, and the stones of the temple anticipated the living stone of Christ, and the living stone of Christ forms us into his image, and we too become living stones:

> As you come to him, a living stone rejected by men but in the sight of God chosen and precious, you yourselves like living stones are being built up as a spiritual house, to be a holy priesthood, to offer spiritual sacrifices acceptable to God through Jesus Christ. (1 Pet. 2:4–5)

This spiritual house is the Most Holy Place where God's holiness was most concentrated and his glory most vivid. The apostle Paul gives a more detailed look:

> You are no longer strangers and aliens, but you are fellow
> citizens with the saints and members of the household of
> God, built on the foundation of the apostles and prophets,
> Christ Jesus himself being the cornerstone, in whom the
> whole structure, being joined together, grows into a holy
> temple in the Lord. In him you also are being built together
> into a dwelling place for God by the Spirit. (Eph. 2:19–22)

Christ is the essential cornerstone, those who taught us Christ
are the foundations, and we are the living stones—a work in
progress until Jesus fully unites heaven and earth.

In another letter, Paul uses temple imagery again when he
writes, "Do you not know that you [as the church] are God's
temple and that God's Spirit dwells in you? (1 Cor. 3:16). Later,
he uses the same image to describe individual saints:

> Do you not know that your body is a temple of the Holy
> Spirit within you, whom you have from God. You are not
> your own, for you were bought with a price. So glorify
> God in your body. (1 Cor. 6:19–20)

"Not your own," "glorify"—the description of a truly human
person is filled with the language of the temple and holiness
on display.

You are among the living stones that comprise God's dwelling on earth and are even a walking temple. So it isn't surprising that as you dwell in Christ by faith, you also look like the
other features of God's house:

> You are a living sacrifice (Rom. 12:1).
> You received living, cleansing water and are a spring of
> living water to others (John 4:14).
> You are the light of the world (Matt. 5:14).
> You have always been the showbread that was kept close
> to God (Ex. 25–30).

Your prayers are the incense, the smoke and aroma of which come before the Lord (Rev. 8:3).

As you move further in and arrive in the Most Holy Place, the images become more of Christ and less of us. When you peer into the treasure chest of God, the ark itself, you find manna and the stone tablets with God's words written on them. These are Christ our food and Christ the speech of God to us.

Living stones to flowing fountains. Living stones stir up images of the Jerusalem temple in all its reflective beauty. Living stones also come from a slightly different lineage of stones, which yield water. The exodus from Egypt and the wilderness years are framed by two events of such living stones. In the first year the people complained of thirst; Moses was instructed to strike a rock, and water came out for the people to drink (Ex. 17:5–6). In the fortieth year nothing had changed; the people still grumbled and complained against the Lord, and he gave them water from a rock. This time, however, Moses was instructed to speak to the living rock rather than strike it, as if the more personal identity behind the rock was being revealed. Moses, instead, in his frustration with the people, struck it twice. Water came out, but Moses's disobedience was the reason he was not allowed to enter the Promised Land.

Ezekiel saw this flowing stone in the temple. He was among the exiles in Babylon who witnessed the destruction of Jerusalem's temple. His message was that God was over the nations, and his plan to be with his people would not be overturned by any earthly kingdom. God would dwell among his people. In a vision Ezekiel invites us to the heavenly temple, where the "water was issuing from below the threshold of the temple toward the east" (Ezek. 47:1). From the stones of the Most Holy Place came the water of life. The water leaked out of the temple and became a fuller, deeper stream that brought life to everything it touched.

The story picks up again at the Feast of Tabernacles—a Hebrew feast open even to Gentiles (Deut. 31:12). During the seven-day festival the people remembered that although they had lived in temporary housing during their time in the wilderness, God himself had cared for them when they could do nothing to provide for themselves. One way he cared was by giving them an ongoing supply of water. With this in mind, each day of the festival began with the priests drawing water from the pool of Siloam and pouring it out by the altar. On the last day the water-drawing festival reached it zenith, with more water and ceremony than on any of the previous days:

> On the last day of the feasts, the great day, Jesus stood up and cried out, "If anyone thirsts, let him come to me and drink. Whoever believes in me, as the Scripture has said, 'Out of his heart will flow rivers of living water.'" Now this he said about the Spirit, whom those who believed in him were to receive. (John 7:37–39)

Jesus is the stone that gives living water. As we believe in him, we are reborn of "water and the Spirit" (John 3:5) and are remade into living temple stones that are so filled with the presence of God that we cannot contain his work in us. It seeps out and brings life to family, friends, neighbors, and the world.

Response

Life has become central to the priestly story. It simply happens when you are close to the Lord, even if you are a rock. The challenge is that death still surrounds us to the point where true life can be obscured. So as you retrain your eyes to the life of Christ in your everyday life, you should expect to see it every day:

- Somebody asks for prayer.
- You are convicted of how you wronged someone, and you ask forgiveness.

- You read Scripture, and it gradually brings you into reality.
- You are thankful for your blessings in Jesus, even when life is not quite right.
- You reach out to someone different from you.

Take time to identify some of the appearances of this water of life, even as it seeps out of you.

35

Enter In

We know that God's Lamb has been sacrificed for us, and the altar has been retired. But the priestly desire to imitate and be like Jesus only grows, so we ask, *Is there any way we can enter into what Jesus did as the pleasing sacrifice?* And there are ways.

Love has become the sacrifice that we bring to the Lord. When we do good and are generous to those in need, we offer a pleasing sacrifice to the Lord (Phil. 4:18; Heb. 13:15). Love was the intent of the sacrificial system all along. To obey the Lord in love has always been preferable to rote, impersonal sacrifice (1 Sam. 15:22–23). So when it comes to priestly sacrifice, Paul, in keeping with his emphasis on our intense closeness with Jesus Christ, makes it about the offering of oneself:

> I appeal to you therefore, brothers, by the mercies of God, to present your bodies as a living sacrifice, holy and acceptable to God, which is your spiritual worship. (Rom. 12:1)

The passage follows a now predictable pattern. God acts first. He gives new mercies in Christ. God makes promises and keeps them, and his faithfulness is not determined by ours. He always acts first and loves the most. Then we respond to his mercy. It just makes sense. Jesus is God's Lamb. Our "spiritual worship" is to be a living sacrifice. This verse could be translated, "This is your proper act of worship as rational people."[23] If we accurately understood God's mercy, we would gladly live for him. Any sane person could do nothing else.

This devotion to the Lord is worked out in the details of everyday life. It includes how we work together as the body of Christ, each exerting the gifts God has given without jealousy or envy, all of which can be summarized as love that is genuine, generous, humble, and persistent even when mistreated.

You can see it if you look. In the last week, I have seen it in a woman who regularly beautifies the building where I work with cut flowers from her garden, all perfectly arranged. Her disappearing mason jars, which are her vases, seem to be an inconsequential loss. I have also seen a spouse falsely accused by family members and wrestling with one question: "How can I show patience and kindness?" Both of these are sane and beautiful sacrifices.

We wash at the basin. The cleansing basin comes next. I once worked in an elementary school where a student smelled like nothing I have ever smelled. We tried brushing his teeth, washing him, taking him to the school nurse, and visiting his home, where the adult who answered the door refused to talk. Despite all our efforts, he emanated a wretched odor that separated him from all his classmates. Children tend to be open about such things: "Yuck, you stink! Get away from me." To be dirty is to be rejected. To be clean, both in Scripture and now, is to be accepted into general society. So we wash. Our daily spiritual washing is our confession of sin, and it should feel something like a cool shower after a day of sweaty, grimy work. We should feel refreshed.

That, of course, can happen only when we remember that we walked by the altar and have been washed thoroughly by the blood of Jesus. Paul wants us to refuse to tolerate personal ungodliness; he also wants us not to tolerate past condemnation and old regrets. So in the most resolute of ways, he heaps on us what has been accomplished in Jesus through the Spirit. The washing has been done to us and for us:

> But you let yourself be washed; but you were set apart; but you have been placed in right relationship with God. All this was accomplished in the name of Jesus in the Spirit of God. (1 Cor. 6:11 AT)

The terms—"washed" and "sanctified" are priestly. The phrase "placed in right relationship" conveys a legal finality. Altogether the verse unequivocally identifies a movement from earth to heaven, and it is the Lord who has done this. The image of letting ourselves be washed is of priestly robes, washed by blood, that are suitable for life in God's presence (Rev. 7:14).

So when you come to the basin, you are not repeatedly coming to Jesus for admittance to his house. "The one who has bathed does not need to wash, except for his feet, but is completely clean" (John 13:10). You come because priests still sin. Though you have been set apart by God for himself, relationships can still be affected by unconfessed sin. So you confess daily, and confession enhances open and close fellowship.

There is a certain knack to feeling clean. The trick is that saints have to understand that their feet really were smelly and dirty. The heroes of the New Testament knew they had been cleansed and forgiven for much (e.g., Luke 7:36–50). Sin is not good, but to know that we are sinners who have been washed in Christ is a great gift.

We light incense, and the smoke comes before the Lord. Now on to the Holy Place where we maintain the censors that burn incense. In God's house there is lots of talking. That's what families do. When you are needy, live among needy people, and live with your generous Father, you talk all the more. We pray, he responds with words from Scripture. Silence and home simply do not go together.

> Let my prayer be counted as incense before you,
>> and the lifting up of my hands as the evening sacrifice!
>> (Ps. 141:2)

Picture bowls. Golden bowls. Our prayers are placed in these bowls, and they are offered to the Lord, along with the prayers of other saints (Rev. 5:8; 8:3). Angels sometimes bring these prayers before the Lord. Angels do not function as long-distance couriers, because we pray to the Lord in his very house. He is with us. Angelic attendants are involved because this is the nerve center of heaven. Heaven acts in response to the prayers of God's people.

This glimpse of spiritual realities gives new zeal to priestly prayers. God, indeed, hears the prayers of one, solitary child who has been abandoned. He also is pleased when the bowls are full. This is why we ask other people to pray. With our more desperate prayers, we ask as many people to pray as possible, and not one prayer is inconsequential to the resulting heavenly aroma.

The old rhythm of temple life is still recognizable. But now we live in God's house; we pass an altar that offered God's lamb, and we can rest. It is in that rest that we go into the world and represent Jesus.

Response

1. What captures your attention from this New Testament walk though the tabernacle?

2. How will you respond?

36

Be Sent Out

The plan had always been that priests would meet in the staging area of God's house in order to be sent out into the world. His house is a place of rest, yet it is also very busy. It is life with a purpose. Following are elements of that mission.

Do battle. Priests were an integral part of Israel's warfare. The first battle in the Promised Land was against Jericho, where the priests brought the ark, and for six days their trumpets were the only sound that could be heard. This was a forerunner of our modern warfare.

We certainly have enemies galore. God's people are martyred every day; those with power use it to satisfy themselves and destroy others (e.g., Ezek. 34:1–6). But we know better than to keep an eye out just for swords and guns. Strategic warfare always aims for the source. We are looking for the world or what is earthly (1 John 2:16; James 3:15), what is from below rather than above. These agents of death are demonic, with Satan behind it all. Look for broken relationships, anger, and quarrels (James 4:1–10). Look for selfish ambition, jealousy, life outside God's safe boundaries, arrogance, and pride. All these things can be found in each of us.

When do we think that sin is not that bad?

When do we think that God is not that good?

When do we think that we are beyond forgiveness and that closeness to God is a dream?

We start with the battle within. Just keep track of your tongue or arrogance that quietly judges from a place above others or personal desires that cast off restraint. Look for anything that you prefer others not to see.

Anger in its manifold variations is singled out for careful guard. Satan is a murderer who has declared war against all who claim allegiance to Jesus (John 8:44; Rev. 12:17). When he sees unleashed anger, he sees images of himself, and there is an opportunity for influence (Eph. 4:27). Anger is not the only sin for which we do battle, but since anger and related divisive sins are such an accurate reflection of Satan, they enlist our complete attention.

Once identified, the battle strategy is clear and detailed. We turn from Satan and turn to the Lord:

> Submit yourselves therefore to God. Resist the devil, and he will flee from you. Draw near to God, and he will draw near to you. Cleanse your hands, you sinners, and purify your hearts, you double-minded. Be wretched and mourn and weep. Let your laughter be turned to mourning and your joy to gloom. Humble yourselves before the Lord, and he will exalt you. (James 4:7–10)

Having entered the battle against our arrogant desires, we turn to the community of Christ. Are there factions? Are members unreconciled? Is there anything that divides? These all receive the encouragement of the evil one and are evidence of death. They must be resisted and laid aside. Priests *discern the body of Christ* (1 Cor. 11:29), which means that we know that the body of Christ is set apart for unity through humility and love, and we work for peace and reconciliation when we see interpersonal fractures.

The battle then is taken to the world in ways that are counterintuitive, sometimes hard yet suitable for human beings. We hope to fit in by being good neighbors who contribute to the good of the community, and we hope to stand out in the way we love. When we encounter the inevitable relationship hassles, this is our opportunity to shine. We are to bless those who persecute us, rejoice with those who rejoice, and weep with those who weep. We are not to be haughty. Instead, we are to associate with the lowly. We are to repay no one evil for evil, and so far as it depends on us, we are to live peaceably with all. We are not to be overcome by evil but to overcome evil with good (see Rom. 12:14–21).

Pray and bless. Through all this we have a keen sense that we need what only God himself can give. How can we stand against temptation? How can we even be *aware* of temptations? How do we love when relationships seem unbalanced, when we receive little but are asked to give more? What are the needs of our neighbors, our community, our world? The life of God's saints in his highly personal creation is one of prayer.

This is an extension of the normal back and forth that characterizes growing relationships: God speaks to us, especially through his word, and we speak from our hearts to him. As we move out into the world, we search for the concerns of earth and bring them to heaven. It begins simply. Our neighbor is sick, and we pray for healing. As we grow, prayer requires more thought. What does our neighbor truly need, and what are the relevant promises of God?

We want to rejoice with those who rejoice and celebrate our neighbor's joys, yet it is trouble that captures our attention.

Troubled circumstances are occasions to serve with rides, food, and other creative ways of care. They are also occasions when we can actually pray with a neighbor.

During trouble, most people welcome prayer. They might think prayer is silly during easier times, but real humanity emerges especially in difficulties, when they are grateful that we pray for them and have them on our hearts. Yesterday I visited a man who had repaired some of our furniture in the past. What began as a general conversation about his life progressed to talk of his encroaching physical struggles, and I prayed for him. Now he expects me to pray when I see him, and he usually cries when I do. We are friends. Stories like this are common and among the most powerful ways that God uses ordinary means to expand his kingdom.

The partner of prayer is blessing. We bless when we have heard the good words spoken in heaven and want to pass them on to those on earth. The Lord blessed us in the beginning (Gen. 1:28). The last words of Jesus before his ascension were a blessing: "He led them out as far as Bethany, and lifting up his hands he blessed them" (Luke 24:50). And those blessings continue, to which are added new mercies and blessings every day.

To speak blessing, we must know God's blessings. Some are unmistakable:

Grace and peace to you (e.g., 2 Pet. 1:2)

May the Lord deal kindly (Ruth 1:8)

May the Lord give you peace (2 Thess. 3:16)

May the Lord direct your hearts to the love of God and to the steadfastness of Christ (2 Thess. 3:5).

Blessed is the one whose transgression is forgiven,
    whose sin is covered. (Ps. 32:1)

Then we speak creative variations on these blessings. We join with the Lord in wanting his favor to be obvious to others. We want the richest of life for them. We might even prepare words to offer the bereaved or to pray over our friends and family. As we bless, we consider the physical and move to the spiritual, which is even more real and enduring.

Blessings mature as we go through Scripture. In the history of Israel, blessings often included offspring and land. Once Jesus came in the flesh, blessings became decidedly spiritual and more enduring. The blessings in the Sermon on the Mount all follow this pattern of heavenly blessings. We, too, mature in order to understand that spiritual blessings are greater than land and offspring. Spiritual realities are the fulfillment of the physical blessings; Christ himself is the fulfillment of the older blessing. He is our safe hiding place, our land at peace.

Spiritual blessings are not a bait-and-switch, in which we hoped for one thing but were given something lesser. Spiritual blessings are from the Spirit. They are certain and permanent in contrast to things that fade and die. So we go back to our predecessors who had no land but had the Lord, who witnessed God's forgiveness of sins that made the way for us to come close.

We easily identify blessings of the Old Testament kind—health, financial security, and other pleasant circumstances. All good things, indeed, come from the Lord. He brings the rain on those who follow him and those who don't. Yet these good things are accompanied by risks. Human beings can too quickly drift from circumstancial blessings into self-sufficiency and a sense of entitlement. Only the deeper blessings are able to sustain us in the leaner years.

Blessed is the one you choose and bring near,
   to dwell in your courts!

We shall be satisfied with the goodness of your house,
  the holiness of your temple! (Ps. 65:4)

Then after going out into the world, sent by the Lord yet also with his presence, we invite others to come near to him and return to his house where together we bless him:

Come, bless the LORD, all you servants of the LORD,
  who stand by night in the house of the LORD!
Lift up your hands to the holy place
  and bless the LORD! (Ps. 134:1–2)

Response

1. Saints rest in Christ, then move out into the world in order to bless. What blessings has the Lord spoken over you that lead you into his rest?

2. How might you bless others?

37

Walking Uphill

The psalms were first used in the morning and evening services of the temple. Most of them are best understood against that backdrop. Here is one of those psalms—Psalm 23. It follows the journey of God's saints and reminds us that God is close:[24]

> The LORD is my shepherd; I shall not want.
>   He makes me lie down in green pastures.
> He leads me beside still waters.
>   He restores my soul.
> He leads me in paths of [his] righteousness
>   for his name's sake.

In spring, during the first month of the Jewish calendar, the month of Passover, the people remember God's deliverance from slavery. It is the only time the land is green.

Among the names Jesus took was that of Good Shepherd, and the very beginning of the psalm points to this. He speaks to us of this role especially when we feel vulnerable and weak. Jesus the shepherd is with us, always close. With sins forgiven, there is nothing that can separate us from his love. We have no reason to be jumpy. We have everything we need, and the waters are quiet rather than turbulent. We are refreshed by him and in him.

When late spring came, so did the Feast of Weeks or Pentecost, when both the harvest and the giving of the law on Mount Sinai were celebrated. We remember when the Spirit was given to us. The Spirit assures us of the presence of Jesus, and he gives us power to follow him during trouble—and there will be trouble. Those reminders strengthen us. It is time to get up. The spring grasses are fading, and we are being led to other grazing places. Wherever we go, we can trust him. He will keep his promise to be with us. He will be faithful to us because he is righteous, and he will take us on the right paths.

> Even though I walk through the valley of the shadow
> of death,
> I will fear no evil,
> for you are with me;
> your rod and your staff,
> they comfort me.

Summer has come and with it the dry season. We are going down. Jesus takes us into the wilderness and its endless dangers. The heat is more intense. All we can do is trust him to know the way, which he does. There are some springs in the desert. The centerpiece of the journey falls here. Though none of the three great festivals appear on the summer calendar, and perhaps because there are no explicit reminders of God during these arid months, we say, "You are with me." Notice the change of voice. We were speaking *about* Jesus; now we speak *to* him. We see his rod and his staff. One protects us from attacks, and the other keeps us from wandering or picks us up when we fall.

You prepare a table before me
    in the presence of my enemies;
you anoint my head with oil;
    my cup overflows.
Surely goodness and mercy shall follow me
    all the days of my life,
and I shall dwell in the house of the Lord
    forever.

Back in the psalmist's day, the heart of the festival season arrived when summer gave way to fall. It was time to walk up Mount Zion and into God's house. The Songs of Ascent (Psalms 120–134) turned their various conversations into one voice of corporate worship and thanks.

First came the Day of Atonement. This time of repentance was solemn yet with the distinct awareness of forgiveness and sins taken far away from the Lord. Immediately following the Day of Atonement was the Feast of Tabernacles or Booths, when the people remembered God's care for them in the wilderness. It was marked by celebration and joy, and it lasted a week.

The image of the shepherd and sheep gives way to the image of the Lord as host, and he has prepared a lavish banquet. His hospitality begins with the anointing of the head with oil, which was customary with honored guests, but this anointing doubles as anointing to the royal priesthood.

The enemies who sought to destroy us are on the outside. They are unclean and cannot enter; we have been made holy and belong. All they can do is watch and absorb the irony of how the ones they cursed are the ones most blessed. We are now in God's house, close to him and enjoying his divine hospitality. He surrounds us. He leads us in his goodness and mercy, and he pursues us in his goodness and mercy. This is humanity as God intended.

Then the calendar turns. We go through the seasons again, and then again. With each year we might be less surprised by the journey through the rocky crags amid dangerous animals. Hope grows even in the wilderness. We say to the Lord, "You are with me," with more confidence. We ask someone near to us for help, or perhaps we take heart in the psalms we sing. Our destination is always God's house, which he has actually prepared for us, so it is our house. It has always been that way. For now, you can pray for endurance and eyes to see these spiritual realities. One day, we will stay put.

Response

1. "You are with me"—all the promises of God orbit around this fact. Every passage on fear is resolved here. God's presence is *the* distinguishing feature of the Christian life. No other gods are inclined to spend their time with human beings, let alone be this close. Do you believe this? Do you need help with your unbelief?

2. Enter into the psalm. What do you see? What do you hear? How would you pray the psalm?

38

The High Priest Prays for You

The journey has its challenges, and the saint's job description is more than you can handle, so Jesus Christ continues in *his* priestly ways. Your high priest prays to the Father for you, and he is joined by the Spirit, who also intercedes for you right now (Rom. 8:26–27).

> [Jesus] holds his priesthood permanently, because he continues forever. Consequently, he is able to save to the uttermost those who draw near to God through him, since he always lives to make intercession for them. (Heb. 7:24–25)

Jesus's longest-recorded prayer has been called the high priestly prayer (John 17). After praying that the Father would glorify the Son in his crucifixion, Jesus prayed for his disciples; then he prays for you. He prays that you would be united with both God and each other in love. This is all very close. It is the heavenly pattern brought into earth, and it is the prominent way the world will know that Jesus was, indeed, from the Father.

> I do not ask for these only, but also for those who will believe in me through their word, that they may all be one, just as you, Father, are in me, and I in you, that they also may be in us, so that the world may believe that you have sent me. (John 17:20–21)

"That they also may be in us"—God's love gathers you into himself. God is one, you are called to live in him and participate in his love, and then you are sent out to express this in daily life through your unity with others. Love and closeness is the life of God's saints. Imagine how a branch abides in the vine (John 15:1–8). You believe in Jesus, which means you have life. Now remain in him by imitating and obeying his love, which takes a lower place and serves. In this way, love is reproduced and expands even more. Jesus prays this once, then he prays it again:

> The glory that you have given me I have given to them, that they may be one even as we are one, I in them and you in me, that they may become perfectly one, so that the world may know that you sent me and loved them even as you loved me. (John 17:22–23)

The small addition is the word *glory*, which Jesus spoke of earlier in his prayer. *Glory* is holiness on full display. It is big, stunning. You cannot look away from it. Imagine Jesus, ordinary-looking one moment, wrapped in light the next, the disciples thunderstruck and left quasi-coherent (Matt. 17:1–8). Glory provoked Moses to seek the face of God, and it evokes the first tabernacle when God's glory descended on it and he dwelled with his people. One with the Father, Son, and Spirit, and, as a result, one with each other—this is glory.

The prayer concludes with what you have come to expect: your purpose is to be near to God, to live with him in his house and to experience his divine hospitality:

Father, I desire that they also, whom you have given me, may be with me where I am, to see my glory that you have given me because you loved me before the foundation of the world. (John 17:24)

A common experience among God's people is, "I know people were praying for me." If we actually ask people to pray for us, and we stay alert to what God does, we should expect this.

- A meeting with a contentious person went better than we had hoped.
- We listened rather than reacted.
- We were able to get what we needed [though not always what we wanted].

Yet there are times when no friend knows or prays, and hardships are kept private. We can know, then, that the Spirit and the Son know our spirit and speak on our behalf to the Father. You can say, "I know that Jesus was praying for me, and I know the Spirit was praying for me." Their prayers are among those gathered in the bowls of incense that came before the Father.

Response

1. Do you believe that Jesus and the Spirit pray for you?

2. What does it mean that you are destined for oneness with the triune God?

Epilogue

The Early Church

The Christian church has not always known what to do with the priesthood of all believers. At first, the teaching about it seems simple. We are all members of the body of Christ. We bring a diversity of gifts that have been given by Christ. The less visible gifts receive special honor. And all this is joined together through love that is interested in others more than in oneself (1 Cor. 12–13). But we bring our own sins. We favor those who can bless us, so we favor the wealthy over the poor. And who doesn't want to be first among equals?

As the church spread, local congregations had particular emphases and put their own spin on the applications of the gospel. In the name of unity, we can easily imagine a more centralized and powerful group that would specify the boundaries for faith and practice. Added to that was a church structure. Elders, overseers, and pastors were appointed to serve (Acts 14:23; Titus 1:5). The body of Christ acknowledged their character and growth in godliness. Though they were clearly servants and not masters, they served in a particular office or calling that was different from the calling of others. Questions certainly arose over the extent of their authority. These were the ingredients for a fractured church.

A moment stands out when Cyprian of Carthage (195–258) presented a church structure that relied on both Roman political traditions and Scripture. He suggested that only a man with the title of bishop could administer the Eucharist, or Lord's Supper. Since the Eucharist was so central to church worship, the new practice gave immediate control to a particular group.[25] Soon, the name *priest* was not for all believers but only for a carefully fenced group with religious and political power.

Martin Luther was largely responsible for retrieving the doctrine of the priesthood of all believers. In booklets such as *Address to the Nobility of the German Nation* (1520), Luther took a stand against the self-proclaimed authority of the pope and how the ordained priests had somehow risen to a category that was different from the universal priesthood. He wrote that those in church office should come from the church community and serve by community consent and election. Furthermore, those who serve are not unique mediators between God and believers. Rather, they equip the congregation for every-member ministry (Eph. 4:1–12).

The resulting landscape generated everything from Catholics to Quakers, with every denomination and local church reckoning with how to describe the work of church officers and individual members. But we can be confident of this: the Spirit has been given to all followers of Jesus, and God is pleased to use ordinary, unassuming men and women to advance his kingdom into our hearts and the world. Scripture is unfamiliar with a passive laity that leaves the work of ministry to ordained professionals. As saints, together we enjoy God's fellowship, we want to know him even better and love him more, and we want those who are further away to come near.

Looking Ahead

The end will come as no surprise. It has been embedded in the story all along. The distance between heaven and earth has always been shorter than we expected. There were always ladders from which the Lord descended, mountains that we ascended, and temples where the throne room was separated by only a curtain. There was always the personal God who spoke to his people and listened to them. He came close and, with certain stipulations, invited us to come close to him. Then Jesus came to earth, and God was here to stay. Jesus was both of heaven and earth, which meant that the plan had always been to *unite* heaven and earth in him. In Jesus Christ, God executed his plan "to unite all things in him, things in heaven and things on earth" (Eph. 1:10).

The garments of the high priest pointed to the fact that God would somehow dwell in his people. Along the way, humanity's clothes gathered some variety. They would get dirty and could be washed only by God himself. They could be altered into the clothes of a divine messenger, or battle garments, or royal robes, or the linen of everyday priests, or sackcloth, and, finally, the garment of a bride. Through all the alterations, the garments retained elements of the priestly pattern, and they always identified how man could draw near to God as he draws near to man.

Now we wait for the fullness of the Most Holy Place to appear—heaven itself, a perfect square, immense (Rev. 21:15–17). God's earthly house was a miniature version of heaven. The heavenly house will come down and infuse earth in a way that the earth itself will shine, full of God's light and overflowing with his life. There will be nothing unclean and no hints of death. Even our everyday pots will be holy to the Lord (Zech. 14:20). What we now know in part, we shall know fully, even as we have been fully known (1 Cor. 13:12). We will see him face-to-face. The Spirit will bring us fully into the Father and the Son, and we will hear, "Behold, the dwelling place of God is with man. He will dwell with them, and they will be his people, and God himself will be with them as their God" (Rev. 21:3).

> But you are a chosen race, a royal priesthood, a holy nation, a people for his own possession, that you may proclaim the excellencies of him who called you out of darkness into his marvelous light. (1 Pet. 2:9)

Response

I have been thinking about the saintly themes of *being closer* and *drawing near* for a few years. Here, I think, are some of the effects:

- I pray differently and pray more often. The Lord is so close that he hears my thoughts. *That* is quite personal and close. Prayer, as a result, has become more natural.
- I have been studying the psalms. They are examples of how we talk to the Lord.
- I have new zeal for obedience. Obedience to Christ serves the relationship, and who could resist a free, open, and close relationship with the triune God? I don't want to have anything to hide before God or humanity. I am seeing that this is certainly not the way we were intended to live.
- I turn to Christ in my fears with more confidence. I know he is with me. This will no doubt be tested in days to come.
- I am enjoying Scripture more, especially as I better understand the endless references and allusions to tabernacles, sacrifices, temples, and blood.
- I know that Scripture is very clear: God extends his invitation to all with open arms, and we can come to him only through the blood of Jesus.
- I am eager for more personal, closer relationships with others.

- I am confessing sins more frequently. Usually daily. With thanks.

I am amazed that God would want to draw me into his triune relationship. This is so amazing that I need persistent reminders. Jesus's prayer in John 17 is one. There he even prays that we would be included in the closeness that is enjoyed within the Trinity. Another passage is a favorite of many, and for good reason: "Behold, I stand at the door and knock. If anyone hears my voice and opens the door, I will come in to him and eat with him, and he with me" (Rev. 3:20). He invites me to come closer to him. He also persistently raps on my door, patiently waiting through my lukewarm times.

And you?

Thank you for considering these things with me.

Notes

1. King Solomon, 2 Chron. 6:18.
2. Martin Luther, "Word and Sacrament," in *Luther's Works*, vol. 36, ed. Abdel Ross Wentz (Philadelphia: Muhlenberg, 1959), 116.
3. John Calvin, "The Epistles of Paul to the Galatians and Ephesians," in *Calvin's Commentaries*, vol. 41, trans. William Pringle, (Edinburgh: Calvin Translation Society, 1854), Eph. 1:10; 205.
4. Julian Barnes, *Nothing to Be Frightened Of* (New York: Vintage, 2008), 3.
5. Michael Morales, *Who Shall Ascend the Mountain of the Lord?* (Downers Grove, IL: InterVarsity Press, 2015), 18.
6. Julie Canlis, *Calvin's Ladder* (Grand Rapids, MI: Eerdmans, 2010), 54.
7. See John Walton, *The Lost World of Genesis One* (Downers Grove, IL: InterVarsity Press, 2009); G. K. Beale and Mitchell Kim, *God Dwells Among Us: Expanding Eden to the Ends of the Earth* (Downers Grove, IL: InterVarsity Press, 2014), chaps. 1–2; also see John Walton, *The Lost World of Adam and Eve: Genesis 2–3 and the Human Origins Debate* (Downers Grove, IL: InterVarsity Press, 2015), 104–15; Uche Anizor and Hank Vos, *Representing Christ: A Vision for the Priesthood of All Believers* (Downers Grove, IL: InterVarsity Press, 2016).
8. See William N. Wilder, "Illumination and Investiture: The Royal Significance of the Tree of Wisdom in Genesis 3," *Westminster Theological Journal* 68 (2006): 51–69.
9. Douglas Green, previously from Westminster Theological Seminary and now Queensland Theological Seminary, is the one who first proposed this alternative reading to me.
10. Exodus 4:24–26 has similarities to this passage. The Lord "met" Moses and was going to put him to death most likely because his family had not been set apart to the Lord by circumcision. The apostle Paul identifies two similar times in his own life. He experienced some wrestling with God before his conversion (Acts 26:14), and he had wrestled in prayer in the midst of affliction (2 Cor. 12:6–10).

11. William R. Millar, *Priesthood in Ancient Israel* (St. Louis, MO: Chalice, 2001), 86.
12. John A. Davies, *A Royal Priesthood* (New York: T & T Clark, 2004). Davies' book argues for a collective royal priesthood.
13. Discussions of tabernacle symbolism can be found in many places. This particular comment about nonverbal prayers comes from Vern Poythress, *The Shadow of Christ in the Law of Moses* (Phillipsburg, NJ: P&R, 1991), 22—a fine exposition of the tabernacle details.
14. For more detail see chapter 2 from Meredith G. Kline, *Images of the Spirit* (Grand Rapids, MI: Baker, 1980).
15. Morales, *Who Shall Ascend the Mountain of the Lord?*, 217.
16. This stone will reappear in Rev. 7:3; 14:1; 22:4.
17. See Meredith Kline, *Glory in Our Midst: A Biblical-Theological Reading of Zechariah's Night Visions* (Eugene, OR: Wipf & Stock, 2001), 122–23.
18. Kline, *Glory in Our Midst*, 127.
19. See J. Daniel Hays, *The Temple and the Tabernacle: A Study of God's Dwelling Places from Genesis to Revelation* (Grand Rapids, MI: Baker, 2016), 63–103.
20. The passage in John is translated as "dwelt among us" (ESV), "took up residence" (HCSB), and "moved into the neighborhood" (Message).
21. Tom Wright, *John for Everyone, Part 1* (Louisville, KY: Westminster John Knox, 2004), 21.
22. Sinclair Ferguson, *The Holy Spirit* (Downers Grove, IL: InterVarsity Press, 1996), 30.
23. Richard N. Longenecker, *The Epistle to the Romans*, in New International Greek Testament Commentary, ed. I. Howard Marshall and Donald A. Hagner (Grand Rapids, MI: Eerdmans, 2016), 920.
24. My setting forth the seasons of Psalm 23 follows the work of Douglas J. Green, "'The Lord Is Christ's Shepherd': Psalm 23 as Messianic Prophecy," in *Eyes to See, Ears to Hear: Essays in Honor of Alan Groves*, ed. Peter Enns, Douglas J. Green, and Michael B. Kelly (Phillipsburg, NJ: P&R, 2010), 33–46.
25. Uche Anizor and Hank Voss, *Representing Christ*, 60–62. Also see Cyril Eastwood, *The Royal Priesthood of the Faithful: An Investigation of the Doctrine from Biblical Times to the Reformation* (Eugene, OR: Wipf & Stock, 2009).

General Index

Aaronic blessing, 107–8
Aaronic priesthood, 61, 65, 98, 142
Abiathar, 66
Abigail, as priest, 56
"abomination that makes desolation," 119
Abraham, 54, 131, 155
abundant life, 28
Adam, to keep guard of the garden, 37, 38
Alexander the Great, 119
altar of incense (tabernacle), 80–81, 82
altars, 53
anger, 192
animal sacrifices, 46, 47, 92, 81, 97, 153–54
animal skins, 46
anointing, 97
Antiochus Epiphanes, 119
ark of the covenant, 82, 117
aroma, sweet and pleasing to the Lord, 82
atheists, 14

banquet, 77, 199
Barnes, Julian, 14
beauty, beautification, 30, 31, 85, 115
believing in Christ, 145–48
blessing, 53, 98, 100, 106–8, 193–96
blood: of animal sacrifices, 153–54; of Jesus, 134
bronze laver, 81
burning bush, 62, 64, 69
burnt offering, 97, 99, 104

Cain, 47–48
calendar, 197–200
calling, 28
cereal offering, 99
cherubim, 81, 91
Christians, as priests, 14
church, as temple, 92
citizens of heaven, 159, 170
cleansing, 98, 100, 129–30
cleansing basin, 186–88
cleansing water, 134
clean and unclean, 71–74
closeness, longing for, 13
clothing, 29, 46, 85
cloud, 104
common, 69
communion with God, 23, 135
confession of sins, 209
consecration, 72, 97–98
creation: bears God's likeness, 25; order in, 70
Cyprian of Carthage, 205–6

Day of Atonement, 100, 103–5, 153, 154, 199
death: contact with, 47; entrance of, 45
devoted to the Lord, 98, 100
"devoted things," 96
discernment: loss of, 39–40, 42; maturing of, 42–44; between two paths, 34–35
disciples, as priests, 164
divine hospitality, 14, 23, 202–3
drink offering, 99

213

early church, 205
Eden, 21, 22, 26, 33, 47, 48, 79,
    81, 143
Elijah, 107
exodus, 118

face of the Father, 108
fear of death, 158
Feast of Booths, 100, 199
Feast of Firstfruits, 100
Feast of Tabernacles, 182, 199
Feast of Trumpets, 100
Feast of Unleavened Bread, 100,
    131
Feast of Weeks, 159, 198
fellowship with God, 23, 110,
    135
filling the earth, 90–91
firstborn, 69
flowing fountains, 181–82
freewill offering, 99
friendship with God, 64
fruitfulness, 27

garden of God. *See* Eden
giving life, 27, 28
glory, 85, 202
glory of God, 107, 175
goat led into the wilderness, 104
God: assures people of his presence,
    58; goodness of, 40; holiness
    of, 109; as light, 176
golden bowls, 188, 203
Good Shepherd, 197
grain offering, 99
Great Commission, 27, 91
growth in discernment, 36
guards, priests as, 91–93

harvest, 102
Hasmoneans, 119–20
heaven and earth: distance between,
    126; united in Christ, 207
heavenly life, 160
Herod the Great, 120–21
high priest, garments of, 86
high priestly prayer, 201–3
holiness, 135; defined the priest-
    hood, 66; of light of Jesus,
    177; practice and growth in,
    109–10

holy, 53, 69–74, 109–11
holy and common, 71
holy days, 100–105
holy nation, 66
Holy Place, in the tabernacle,
    80–82
Holy Spirit: descent of, 159; hover-
    ing over waters at creation,
    20; keeps us tethered to Christ,
    167; as ways of heaven on
    earth, 167–70
hopelessness, 40
humanity, noble mission of, 27

idol worship, 118
image of God, 25–27
    refashioned into, 116
    restoration of, 86
incense, 188
"in Christ," 156
inheritance, 96, 160
intimacy with God, 14, 31
Isaiah, 154
Israel: divided kingdom, 118; exile
    and return, 118–19; grumbling
    in the wilderness, 177–78; as
    priests, 66
Israel (name), as "prevailer with
    God," 59

Jacob: blessed with new name, 59;
    as deceiver, 59, 126; dream
    of a ladder, 55, 58, 125–26;
    wrestled with God, 57–59
Jesus Christ: ascension of, 158–59;
    baptism of, 130; conquered
    death, 158; as cornerstone,
    180; death of, 153–56, 157;
    descent from heaven, 125,
    149–52, 157, 168; emptied
    himself of power, 58; as high
    priest, 90, 92, 141–43, 201–3;
    humility and gentleness of,
    164; meals with the unworthy,
    77; as new Adam, 155; as
    Passover Lamb, 130–32, 134;
    resurrection of, 157–58; as
    royal branch, 116; as shep-
    herd, 197; tabernacled among
    us, 126; as the temple, 137–38
Job, 37–38, 54

Scripture Index

Also Available from Edward T. Welch

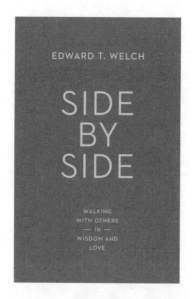

"I have come to rely on Welch for guidance and insight
in better understanding the issues of the soul."
Bob Lepine, Cohost, *FamilyLife Today*

For more information, visit **crossway.org**.

Restoring Christ to Counseling and Counseling to the Church

COUNSELING
ccef.org/counseling

WRITING
ccef.org/resources

TEACHING
ccef.org/courses

EVENTS
ccef.org/events

"CCEF is all about giving hope and help with a 'heart.' If you want to learn how to effectively use God's Word in counseling, this is your resource!"

Joni Eareckson Tada, Founder and CEO, Joni and Friends International Disability Center

"The vision of the centrality of God, the sufficiency of Scripture, and the necessity of sweet spiritual communion with the crucified and living Christ—these impulses that lie behind the CCEF ministries make it easy to commend them to everyone who loves the Church."

John Piper, Founder, desiringGod.org; Chancellor, Bethlehem College & Seminary

Christian Counseling & Educational Foundation
ccef.org